"*God.com* is a refreshing approach to connecting intimately with the most high God. It is a tool to help the reader learn to communicate with God and to learn to hear His voice. It is innocent, poignant, and profound."

PHIL JOEL
RECORDING ARTIST, NEWSBOYS

"James is a man on one of the most incredible quests ever laid out for the human hear—the quest to find ultimate truth in the Ultimate Truth. As you travel with him in this book, I can promise you'll laugh and cry. You'll be astounded and amazed. You've never read anything like this before—and probably never will again. Most of all, you will find that you are not alone in your quest to find the answers that only the one true source of Truth can give."

NORM MINTLE
PRESIDENT, PURE MEDIA COMPANY

"The passion and reality with which James writes underscores his incredible journey of discovery. A discovery of God and with God. We all need to discover who God is and what He wants to be in us. This book will shape your life if you allow your heart to be as open as these pages."

LEO HANSSEN, SENIOR MINISTER,
CITY NEW LIFE CHURCH,
CHRISTCHURCH, NEW ZEALAND

"I'm impressed by the passion with which James Langteaux attacks the idols in life—those barriers that keep us from the actualized lives we're intended to live—and the clarity with which he communicates to his readers how they, too, can resolve to truly hear from God, set their life course, and live in wholeness. This is an honest book."

"DR. LINDA," PSYCHOTHERAPIST,
AUTHOR OF *KIDS KILLING KIDS* AND *GETTING UNSTUCK*,
AND ADJUNCT PROFESSOR, WHEATON COLLEGE
DEPARTMENT OF PSYCHOLOGY

GOD.COM

BECOME INTERACTIVE WITH THE GOD OF THE

UNIVERSE. LOG ON TO HIS PAGE AND YOUR

SOFTWHERE WILL DRAMATICALLY CHANGE.

WHEREVER YOU GO.

GODCom

god.com

XTREME INTIMACY WITH AN INTERACTIVE GOD

Multnomah Publishers® *Sisters, Oregon*

JAMES ALEXANDER LANGTEAUX

GOD.COM
published by Multnomah Publishers, Inc.

© 2000 by James Langteaux
International Standard Book Number: 1-57673-707-1

Cover image of man by David Bailey Photography.
Cover image of wings by Keith Brofsky/Tony Stone Images.
Cover image of eye by PhotoDisc.
Back cover image of angel by Photonica.

Scripture quotations are from:
The Holy Bible, New International Version (NIV) © 1973, 1984 by International Bible
Society, used by permission of Zondervan Publishing House

The Holy Bible, New King James Version (NKJV) © 1984 by Thomas Nelson, Inc.

The Living Bible (TLB) © 1971. Used by permission of
Tyndale House Publishers, Inc. All rights reserved.

The Message © 1993 by Eugene H. Peterson

Multnomah is a trademark of Multnomah Publishers, Inc.,
and is registered in the U.S. Patent and Trademark Office.

The colophon is a trademark of Multnomah Publishers, Inc.

Printed in the United States of America

For information:
MULTNOMAH PUBLISHERS, INC. • P.O. BOX 1720 • SISTERS, OR 97759

Library of Congress Cataloging-in-Publication Data
Langteaux. James Alexander.
God.com: extreme intimacy with an interactive God / by James
Alexander Langteaux.
       p. cm.
       ISBN 1-57673-707-1
       1. Spiritual life—Christianity. I. Title: God dot com. II. Title.
BV4501 .2 .L31813 2000
248.4—dc21
00-008607

00 01 02 03 04 05— 10 9 8 7 6 5 4 3 2 1 0

A DEDICATION...

This book is dedicated to that great cloud of witnesses—those who have gone before in the spirit of true revolution and who were willing to die before ever really seeing. To those who have spoken so boldly into my life after hearing so clearly from the God who wishes to speak: Marian, Cindy, Diane, Anthony, Norm, Jolene, Jon, Nancy, Chris, Aaron, Terry. And to all the rest of you who have been willing to believe—and live like you mean it.

...AND THANKS

Because this book is all about the willingness to risk by believing, I offer a very humble thanks to Don Jacobson, president and publisher of Multnomah, for believing beyond what he could see when we first met (among other things, the word Crazy written in German on the sleeves of my motorcycle jacket). I know that publishing this sort of book is a bit crazy for a publishing house with such a stellar reputation. I can't thank you enough for your willingness to risk. I will never forget the words you've said to me time and time again: "James, you make me uncomfortably comfortable." Thank you, Don, for being bold and uncomfortable—and for making me feel at home in the Multnomah family.

A special thanks to all my new friends and family at Multnomah, from that first random telemarketer who reached me on the rooftop, opening the doors and hearts to the warrior believers in Oregon who made this all possible. Thank you, Doug Robinson, Torrey Sharp, Kevin Marks, Bill Jensen, Ken Ruettgers, Chris Gilbert (your artistry rocks!), the Jeffs (Leeland and Pederson), and Keith Wall, my editor, who looked past my flaws into what could be on the other side of the dream. Extreme gratitude to Judith St. Pierre—my own private St. Jude.

And thanks to my family at home for standing by and loving through the years—for all the training and wisdom and for introducing me to my best friend. And for my new friend, a man I've been dying to get to know–my father. It looks like we have many bowls of cereal ahead of us.

And mostly, thanks G.

FOREWORD

Jame's life, we discover, has been one big quest for love and truth. *God.com* is his confessional. And let me tell you—he bares all. He made me laugh, and on occasion, he made me teary-eyed. He shocked me (me, of all people), and he challenged my doctrine and my own standards of honesty. Above all, he made me think, and for that I am grateful.

To some he will seem crazy (he likes people to think that anyway), but to me, James is a revolutionary who wants people to wake out of the deep and comforable slumber that pervades Western culture—and in particular Christian culture.

This is a book I want my friends to read. To the agnostic it describes the human side of God. To the outcast it is a tale of unconditional love. To the disillusioned it blends wit and honesty to offer hope. To the dreamer it inspires bigger dreams and visions.

God.com is the most thought-provoking book on faith I have ever read. It is not a book for the religious, and yet it is about man's desire to know God. It is not a book for the cynic, and yet it has pages of humorous sideways glances at the Church and our collective beliefs. This is a book about what we truly believe deep down about ourselves, our dreams, our mistakes, and our true feelings about life, love, and God. We can talk about God, ignore God, sing about God, think about God, curse God, or forget about God. But do we dare know God?

READ ON AND FIND OUT.

CHRIS FALSON,
RECORDING ARTIST, SINGER/SONGWRITER, RECORD PRODUCER

MAIN MENU

CHAPTER 1.0
IN THE BEGINNING

AFTERWORDS 2.0
4:01 A.M. AN AWAKENING
WHEN GOD CALLS, IT'S USUALLY WAY TOO EARLY.

AFTERWORDS 2.5
THE SOUNDS OF SILENCE
TURNING OFF. TUNING IN.

AFTERWORDS 3.0
GOD'S OWN SON
GETTING PAST THE PRODIGAL PART.

AFTERWORDS 4.0
DETECTING VIRUSES
BUGS BE GONE WHEN THE BLOOD BEGINS.

AFTERWORDS 4.5
DEATH AND THE WILL
LETTING GO OF YOURS. ACCEPTING HIS.

AFTERWORDS 5.0
LOGGING ON
ACCESSING HIS HOME PAGE—HIS WILL.

AFTERWORDS 6.0
THE TROJAN FORCE
LOVE AND COMPASSION CAN TAKE
YOU BEHIND ENEMY LINES AND WIN
EVEN THE MOST FORTIFIED CITIES.

GOD?COM

God.com is intended to introduce you to the most incredible friend I have come to know. It is meant to show you how, by becoming interactive with the God of the universe, our softwhere will dramatically change—wherever we go.

I hope that this book will speak two languages. On one level, I want to speak to the skeptic who claims not to believe. On the other, I want to challenge those who claim they believe to begin to really live like they mean it.

Although I wrote this book for you, it may have been just as much for me. As much as I thought I believed, in the end the writing of this book has truly set me free.

Now, more than ever, I really do believe.

IF YOU WANT TO BELIEVE,   J U S T A S K

IF YOU BELIEVE, ASK FOR THE ABILITY TO HEAR GOD'S VOICE

IF YOU HEAR, ASK TO LOVE

IF YOU LOVE, ASK TO SHOW YOUR LOVE THROUGH

A WILLINGNESS TO OBEY

IF YOU MOVE IN OBEDIENCE, ASK FOR POWER TO MOVE MOUNTAINS

IF YOU MOVE IN POWER, ASK TO BE USED IN STRATEGY

IF YOU ARE USED IN STRATEGY, ASK FOR THE REST. REAL REST

THEN RETURN TO MAIN MENU AND **B E G I N   A G A I N.**

LOG ON.

IT REALLY IS AN ADDRESS YOU CAN'T FORGET.

As the essence of courage is to stake one's life on a possibility, so the essence of faith is to believe the possibility exists.

WILLIAM SALTER

CHAPTER 1.0
IN THE BEGINNING

BELIEVE.

THE END.

AFTERWORDS

IN THE BEGINNING IS THE WORD

And the word is B E L I E V E.

We are all dying to believe. And dying because we don't. I think believing is a little like looking past what we can see to stare into the eyes of God while falling forward into the blackness—forward, ever forward—free-falling until finally we can see. When we do, what we see is what He sees. BUT ONLY AFTER BECOMING HIS PUPIL.

Falling into blackness is not my idea of fun, especially when I don't know when, where, or how the blackness will finally end. Or, more frighteningly still, if it ever will end.

Belief requires a beginning, and that is where we are.

For me, belief began a few years ago with a falling experience—falling from a comfortable life working for a television network; falling, falling nearly off the planet to learn to listen, obey, and trust.

When the God of the universe asks you to believe, your

response will ultimately depend on where you are standing, because where you are standing will affect what and how you are hearing.

Monty Python made that point in ***The Life of Brian.*** It captured something powerful in the scene where Jesus speaks to the crowd of five thousand. If you think about the logistics of that endeavor in light of the lack of technology, amplification, and lapel mics, you'll realize that there would have been a lot of people who wouldn't have heard exactly what Jesus said. What they heard would have depended on where they were standing. Even though Jesus' words to the crowd were "Blessed are the peacemakers," the guys in the back heard "Blessed are the cheesemakers, for they shall inherit the earth."

"What's so special about cheesemakers?" they asked each other. An argument ensued—as discussions involving God and cheese so often do.

The first time God asked me to believe, I was standing knee-deep in the decadent decade of the '80s. Jesus asked me, just as He asked the rich young ruler, to sell everything, give to the poor, and follow Him. Despite what Jesus said, I heard, "Buy all you can, wave to the poor, and I will follow you."

So I did. And He didn't.

God is patient and loving. He waited a while before He asked me again. He waited until my proximity had improved my ability to hear Him. It took me about seven years of moving closer to be able to heed His call. When He asked again, I heard correctly.

This time, however, selling all I had involved letting go of a comfortable job, world travel, a home, car, and friends and moving ten thousand miles from warmth and safety to the bottom of the planet. In short, I had an opportunity to create a new model for television at a quarter of my salary, at a facility with a fraction of the equipment and resources I was used to, at a two-bit TV station on the south island of New Zealand.

It was glamorous and exciting—right up until I landed in Christchurch and was denied the standard three-month visa. Instead I was given three days. *This can't be a by-product of belief,* I thought. Following that moment of defeat, my new boss dropped me off at a cold, dreary motel, and through cloudy eyes and with a misty mind, I watched a dark sky begin to gently weep. After twenty-four hours of flying forward and flailing faithwise, I found myself falling fitfully into a dark and dreamless sleep.

Falling off the planet into an abyss called belief is probably the most frightening decision a person could ever choose to make. Maybe that's why the journey called *believe* is one people seldom take.

When I woke disoriented, dazed, and confused, with my internal clock completely askew, I wrestled with waking dreams of my friends in the States, at the pub, near the beach where we used to sit late into the summer nights talking endlessly about life, love, God, and friendship. The camaraderie only intensified when I shared my plans to move to New Zealand. It's funny how people will drop their guard and let their walls fall when they know you are about to leave. Their secrets are safe with you, and they will tell you how much they love you, because you'll soon be gone, and their vulnerability will have no consequences.

But this isn't a story about moving to New Zealand, or anywhere else for that matter. The story of *believe* involves moving all over or nowhere at all, depending on what your unique calling may be. We all have a purpose and a destiny, but we only begin to see it when we let ourselves go falling forward into the dark land of belief. OFTEN IT IS MUCH HARDER TO BELIEVE AFTER YOU TAKE THAT LEAP.

As hard as it may be, this adventure is worth every hardship, doubt, and fear you must wrestle with until you come to that gentle place where you can sleep, nestled close to the one who calls you to believe no matter how the storms rage or the waves threaten.

Will you stare deeply into the eyes of God and look past what you can see? Will you fall forward into the blackness of belief while you flail and fight until you learn to rest in the knowledge that you don't have to see when you truly believe?

I WANT TO BELIEVE.

And I believe you want to, too, or you wouldn't be reading these words. But I don't want to believe that I'm supposed to love a god I've learned to fear, a god I've run from, and a god I don't understand— like some bipolar boyfriend who has suddenly moved in with my mom. Just because she loves him doesn't mean I have to, will, or can.

But what if our preconceived image of God is not the real God? What if He has been misrepresented, misinterpreted, and misplaced? What if the one true God has nearly been erased? What if the God we are longing to know could not be controlled, so another, a phony clone, was placed upon the throne? That way the one who usurped control can remain on-line while the true God waits on hold.

I want to believe that a God who cared enough to create companions would be interested in interacting with His creation. Why would He have begotten children whom He only wished to ignore?

WHATEVER FOR?

It's logical to assume that the God who set our lives in motion would have deep emotion and be consumed by the ocean of tears many of us shed as we make our way on this journey called life.

God is our Father. For some of us, that doesn't help at all because we don't have a healthy understanding of what a father should be and how a father should love. But God is the perfect Father—the mother of all fathers.

He loves us as any good father would love his children. Only more so, because He is God, and He sees from an eternal perspective. He is able to look past the here and now and see the us in the there and then. Our God, our Father, is longing to spend time with us. I don't think He wants us to do all the talking. I think He wants us to give Him room to speak.

BELIEF IS REALLY ONLY THE BEGINNING.

If we really believe, then we will want to do something about it. If we want to discover the truth, we need to find a way to access this God: the true God. Not your god, or my god, or a pleasant potpourri. We need to meet **the** God. The one who is not of our design or making; the one who did the making—the making of you, of me, of our world, and all that we see. We need to log on to His page and become interactive with Him.

IF WE REALLY WANT TO BELIEVE.

Being interactive with the God of the universe requires the simple belief that He is willing and able to speak to us, to become involved in our daily lives, to care enough to send the very best. He does. And He did. That is the hallmark of who He is and why we should believe. This is the unique story of a God who cares about the outsider, the disenfranchised, the underdog. This is the story of a God who was so moved by the pain of His creation that He was willing to become like us to lead us. It cost Him His life. Now all He wants is for us to become like Him so we can lead those who do not believe.

Maybe it's about more than just belief. Maybe the problem has been the *object* of our belief.

"BEWARE OF GOD"

That was not a dyslexic moment. Once when I was working out at the gym, I saw a guy with a goatee wearing a T-shirt that said "Beware of God." The words were huge, bold, and screened in danger red. They screamed danger as I read. I wanted to talk to him and ask him what had prompted him to warn the world of a big, scary God who bites. Then I realized there was nothing strange about that particular man wearing that particular shirt. Many of us wear that warning in one way or another.

Those are the words many of us would use to warn the weary to be wary on their spiritual journey. "Beware of God" captures the wariness we feel on varying levels and to different degrees toward the God who Christians claim has set us free. Free indeed. Why is it, then, that so many of them, so many of us, don't seem to be free?

The God I've heard about sounds like a crabby old man with a lot of outdated rules and laws that keep me from being me—at least who I perceive myself to be. But maybe our "Beware of God" sign should instead read:

"B E W A R E   O F   D O G M A"

IT CAN BE MORE DANGEROUS THAN YOU COULD BELIEVE.

Dogma is our interpretation of God, and interpretations (when they are ours, not His) often become muddled, manipulative, and frighteningly fallible (like us). When that happens, dogma divides. The God of all creation loves and unifies.

Are you willing to take down your "BEWARE OF GOD" sign? A decision like that involves significant risk and a willingness to believe that there is a reason to take it.

Will you risk your reputation, your loves, your money, your will, and your life in order to believe? If not, relax—you seem to have it all under control. But if you are at all like me, and you've come to realize that "your cheese tends to fall off your cracker at fancy cocktail parties" (as an old friend used to say), it couldn't hurt to take that risk.

It is a risk to believe. It isn't safe, and often it isn't fun. It is real and painful. But when you make the leap of faith, astonishing things—things you never could have dreamed—become a powerful part of your waking world. Miracles happen when you risk. When you **believe**. Dead people come alive; ordinary types defy gravity and other assorted natural laws; captives are set free. And God laughs.

He does, you know.

This God is a champion of risk. Who in his right mind would create living beings free to either love or not love their Creator? To trust or not trust; to believe or not to believe?

That is the question.

This God risked all He loved most by giving us the right to choose. This risk even touched His one beloved Son, who told the truth in His living, though the telling meant dying. He risked and He believed. There is nothing safe about either of those things. Laying your life down, naked, on a rough piece of tree only to have those you love hammer you with insults and nine-inch nails takes great belief. And love.

Perfect love. NO FEAR.

It doesn't end there. Jesus believed that His Father was a good Father and had a plan—a death-defying plan with a supernatural twist. If His Father was telling the truth, and that truth included seeing life on the other side of the grave, He had to believe there was a good enough reason to take that risk—*us.* He believed that we were worth dying for. He believed His Father, and He believed in you and me. He continues to believe in us.

HE RISKED, AND WE WON.

THE ODDS ARE APTLY NAMED.

Are you willing to risk it all to believe? Are you willing to lay it all down? It will cost you everything and nothing at the same time. It will turn your life upside down by allowing you to become who you really are in Him. It will allow you to live like Jesus lived while you become who He intended you to be. This involves sacrifice, but when you risk, you win more than the lottery. The dividends are paid out each year for twenty years and then some.

And then sum.

What kind of fool believes?

I'm beginning to believe, and I'm betting you are, too. It's really not as difficult as it may seem. All we really need to do is to ask a couple of questions: God, will you help me believe? Will you help me get past me and my stuff so I can move into You and Yours to see my world and my softwhere dramatically changed? Unrecognizably so? Uncompromisingly so?

If so, log on to begin your search. If you don't ask, you haven't got a prayer. And that's all prayer is—a simple conversation. The wisdom of the world says we should believe only after we see, but the foolishness of God asks us to believe before we really see. Paradoxically, God asks the impossible while moving mightily through the improbable to make even the immovable unstoppable.

Love is not blind. Doubt is. **Believe it or not.**

"I HAVE COME INTO THIS WORLD, THAT THOSE WHO DO NOT
SEE MAY SEE, AND THAT THOSE WHO SEE MAY BE MADE BLIND."

www.john@9.39.com/nkjv

AND THE WORD
BECAME FLESH

WORDSWORDSWOR

At the very beginning of this journey, it is important to rec-
ognize the power that lies dormant in the words that we use and abuse
to plan, to praise, to curse, and to connive.

There is intense power in the Word. One man said the
pen is mightier than the sword. I doubt he was advocating a rumble
with a Rollerball. It's safe to assume he meant words. From the
beginning of time, from the mouth of God, all creative power has
rested in the Word. Everything that was to be was first in Him and in
His Word.

Some things never change. He is the same yesterday,
today, and forever, and His Word remains constant. His Word is lib-
erating and life-giving. When His Words become our words, we too

hold power—power to bring life, healing, and freedom.

His words are the foundation of everything that is and everything that will be. If only we could truly understand the vast power contained in these tiny capsules: His **Words.**

Before there **was,** there **were Words.**

WWW. (WORLD WIDE WORD)

Although believe is just one little word among many, it has great and eternal power. When it comes alive in your life, you naturally begin to see. I mean really see—supernaturally. And sometimes seeing can be more difficult than believing, because once you see, you can never go back. And once you begin to see, you may also begin to hear—voices.

WELL, A VOICE ACTUALLY.

AfterWords 2.0
An Awakening

4:01 A.M.

AN AWAKENING

WHEN GOD CALLS, IT'S USUALLY WAY TOO EARLY.
MAYBE HE FORGETS THE TIME DIFFERENCE.

A Crazy Kind of Early...4:01 A.M.

TURNS OUT, IT'S NOT AN UNGODLY HOUR AFTER ALL!

On September 20, 1995, at 4:01 in the morning, the Most High God of
the universe woke me. It was early, so I don't remember for certain
what I said. But because I was in that land that floats between reality
and dreams, I was softer and more open than I would have been at,
say, midday or at three. I'm pretty sure my reply was something profound—like, "What?"

Strange that a random guy like me would have the honor of
hearing from God at any hour, much less at an hour usually considered
ungodly. But the longer I live, the more I realize that God often works
outside our schedules and that He isn't bound by manmade borders,
titles, corporations, or governments. He is the Government of all. He
makes the rules and sets the clock. When we learn to operate within
His parameters, we see our lives dramatically changed.

GOD'S INTO WAKE-UP CALLS

God is a specialist at turning lives upside down. Many of His recorded wake-up calls were actually emergency line breaks. When a guy named Saul was in the middle of his personal crusade to crucify Christians, God showed up in a blinding display that knocked him out of commission for several days. During that divine diversion, God performed spiritual surgery to align Saul's misguided zeal with the truth of who He is and what He wanted to do in his life. This was not an intervention Saul asked for or wanted.

The unlikely thing about God is that even while we are killing His kids, He responds by killing us with kindness. It's simply not logical. But it is so God.

When you encounter the truth of who God is, no matter what you are into or who you claim to be, you will walk out of your blindness and into the light. With your eyes wide open, you will see who you really are in the light of His love.

Today, like then, God turns Sauls into Pauls and changes crusaders of chaos into champions of the cause. Only the names are changed to protect the ignorant.

THIS IS A GENERATION OF EXTREMES—EXTREME SPORTS, EXTREME LIFESTYLES, AND EXTREME PARADOXES. WHEN extremists encounter the TRUTH, THEY WILL LIVE AND DIE FOR IT. EXTREMELY.

WHOEVER EMBRACES A VICE ENDS UP A SLAVE TO THAT VICE...BUT IF THE SON MAKES YOU FREE, YOU WILL BE FREE—PERIOD.

James paraphrasing John quoting Jesus www.john@ 8.34–36.com

In the world's economy, I am an unlikely candidate to be chosen by God for an early morning conversation. The only credit I can take for it is that one day, in a rather offhanded way, I sort of mentioned that I would like to hear from God. Although there was a big part of me that didn't really believe God would enter my domain, He honored the tiny shred in me that did.

Some things I'm going tell you may alarm you. You may think it's crazy that the God of the universe would wake any of us at a ridiculous hour to share something from His heart. I mean, who are we?

WHO WAS SAMUEL?

If you've heard the story of Samuel, you'll recall that as a young boy he had a direct encounter with the Most High. God had to call him three or four times before Samuel knew that it was God on the other end of the wake-up call. Once he knew he was not the target of a prank phone call, Samuel acted like it was perfectly normal to have a direct line to the Creator of the universe.

Here's the real beauty of the story: Samuel believed. That is all God wants from us anyway—to simply believe as children believe. When we respond with skeptical incredulity, we limit Him and bring Him to our level. And the truth is, He just won't fit on our level. He is far too grand.

AN A.D.D. MOMENT As part of a video project, I've recently been hanging out with gang members in East Los Angeles and Watts. When I asked a sixteen-year-old gang kid how someone can get out of the gang, he replied, "You can't."

In that moment, I learned an important **truth.** If you believe you can be set free—whatever your problem or addiction may be—you will be free. If you believe you cannot, then you will prove yourself right. If we believe the Most High God will break our chains of bondage—to sex, money, fame, drugs, memories, perversions, pride, gossip, hatred, or greed—He will break them, and we will be free. We hold the key—and the key is **belief.**

THE THINGS WHICH ARE IMPOSSIBLE WITH MEN ARE POSSIBLE WITH GOD.

www.luke@18.27.com/nkjv

When we constrain God, we constrain ourselves. By imposing false limitations, we embrace a self-imposed slavery that robs us of our vision and our purpose. And without vision and purpose, people perish.

When we ask God to do the miraculous and muster even a small seed of belief, it will be only a matter of time before our destiny will be dramatically redirected.

I don't know why we act surprised when God enters our domain in a personal and tangible way. Open just about any book in the Old Testament, and you will find account after account of God speaking directly to those who would listen. The God I'm talking about today is the same God who spoke freely with His prophets, His priests, and His kings—even with shepherd boys who liked to sing.

BELIEVE IN THE LORD YOUR GOD, AND YOU SHALL BE ESTABLISHED; BELIEVE HIS PROPHETS, AND YOU SHALL PROSPER.

www.2chronicles@20.20.com/nkjv

He is the same yesterday, today, and forever. Although His mercies are new every morning, His characteristics remain constant. The historical record clearly indicates that God chooses to speak directly into our lives, either supernaturally with a bit of panache—such as talking shrubs—or through a simple wake-up call as recorded in the story of Samuel.

Part of our problem is that we have too many things that occupy our minds, so we can't hear above the din of our daily distractions. If we don't clear some space for God to speak, He'll create a time and place where He can be heard. It might have to be where and when there is no other sound in our head.

But I digress.

At 4:01 that September morning of '95, God followed my weak little *"what?"* with two instructions. There were no introductory remarks, no small talk or pleasantries, just the communication of two things He wanted me to do.

The first was to begin a two-week audiovisual fast—no movies, television, magazines, radio, or music. He wanted me to create an atmosphere of silence into which He could speak. He wanted me to learn to *hear* and *know* His voice. Second, He asked me to take a road trip with Him to Richmond, Virginia, so I could learn to listen and obey.

As strange as it all seemed, I obeyed His instructions. I didn't question, and I didn't drag my feet. Sure, asking my employer for the day off to go to the Confederate capital for no particular reason seemed a little bizarre. But I knew something was up when the people I worked with asked no questions and even suggested that I might "hear from God" on the journey. I was stunned.

I was even more stunned when I actually did hear from God. All day long. I had removed the CD player from the car (all my home noisemakers were neutered as well), so there was none of the normal rattle and hum to occupy my mind. I didn't know where in Richmond I was going—I just knew I was going with the one who made me, and that was good enough.

As I look back, I realize that this trip was the beginning of a journey that has undoubtedly led many people to think I may be crazy. I can just hear their conversations after we've had dinner together: "I'm sure he believes it is all real—poor guy. I'm sure he means well."

If I am crazy, then I can only say that crazy is quite an adventure. And this God I've imagined is more phenomenal than any variety available in the full color spectrum of gods. If I'm right, and God does speak into our lives, then I've entered the bonus round. If I'm wrong…well, I guess I meant well. Whatever that means.

2 WRONGS DON'T MAKE A RELIGIOUS RIGHT.

Many people who claim to be religious tend to have a problem with this sort of talk. It moves them outside of the comfortable little boxes they have designed, and it disables their control mechanisms. I understand why Jesus disparaged the religious of His day while loving all the rest with outrageous and copious quantities of compassion. The religious often try to wrap up God and pack Him away in a neat, tiny box. The problem is that the real God of the universe isn't small or pre-dictable. He's immense. And He's far too powerful to be wrapped and boxed and bagged to go.

Yet God willingly enters the most stifling and repressive of boxes to offer us a divine plan of escape. Out of His unfailing love and unfathomable mercy, He comes to enlighten us—even the religious— and enable us to right our wrongs through His amazing grace.

BOXING GOD

There is no box big enough for my God. He is a great and glorious God. And, quite honestly, He is quite conversational if you give Him the space to speak.

The day of my road trip with God was the best day of my life. While driving north from Virginia Beach, I had an hour-long con-versation with the one who made me. He was funny, engaging, and He seemed to have all the answers to my questions. For the first fifty min-utes, I didn't let myself realize how unusual or extraordinary it was. The conversation was going on in my head. (For those of you wonder-ing it was like a series of thoughts, but stronger and much more focused and direct.) I finally asked God why He used the words that I used and why His sense of humor was so similar to mine. At that point I began to suspect that I might have been making up the entire episode.

But His answer was great. He said that it wouldn't make a lot of sense for Him to speak Chinese to me, since my native tongue is English. (Actually, it is my only tongue.) It would only make sense for Him to speak in my language and in words I was comfortable using. He also said He created my sense of humor, so it was only natural to play off of it.

In that hour-long conversation, I had one other shred of evidence that I wasn't crazy. I am so chronically A.D.D. that there was no way I could have conducted an hour-long conversation with anyone else, much less myself, without distraction.

The real proof came when God said I should go to a coffeehouse I had frequented a few years earlier when I was working on an NBC miniseries in Richmond. He said I would get there at exactly 2:17 P.M. I said, "Okay." But just then I spotted a sign that said Richmond was only seventeen miles ahead. According to my calculations and past experiences, I would get there thirty minutes before God's predetermined arrival time.

I KNEW I WAS CRAZY
I MUST HAVE BEEN MAKING ALL OF THIS UP

But within five minutes, the interstate narrowed to a single lane, and true to God's itinerary, I arrived at exactly 2:17. Now my head was spinning. While I was at the coffeehouse, God explained that this was a day of learning to listen and obey—a day when He would tell me exactly where to go, when to go, and when to leave. I was not to second-guess or slide my own agenda on top of His. This truly would be new for me.

From the coffeehouse He told me to drive to the Hollywood Cemetery. I recalled that I'd been there a few years back during the filming of the miniseries, but I didn't remember where it was. Then I realized that all I had to do was ask for directions. The God of the universe is better and more personal than *Yahoo's* map service. The directions weren't written down; He gave them to me by telling me where I should turn.

When I arrived at the cemetery, at the hour that He indicated, He showed me a mental picture of where I was to sit. It was high atop a peaceful hill, under a giant oak tree, where shafts of sunlight dripped through the leaves, making warm, glowing pools in that garden of the dead. For the record, I avoid cemeteries whenever possible. But as I made my way—actually His way—to the designated spot, I saw tombstone after tombstone with the words "Only the pure in heart shall see God." Those words lit up those grave markers like neon signs. Then the words came into my mind: "There is a reason for that, my son. It is Truth."

I made a note of that. So far, it looked as though I was only going to *hear* God, because my heart was far from pure. But He sees the end from the beginning. Although our hearts may not be pure now, He knows that in time, if we believe, listen, and obey, He will be able to work out all the kinks and wrinkles, scars and stains, leaving us with a heart that is pure. And He will do it by His grace and goodness **alone.**

After a while, in the surreal stillness of that peaceful place, I broke the silence by asking God a question. I had recently seen the movie ***Braveheart,*** and after watching William Wallace wipe out countless Englishmen, I wondered how my other hero, Israel's King David, had been able to slay his thousands and ten thousands in bloody hand-to-hand combat. As I watched the powerful battle scenes so brilliantly recreated in ***Braveheart,*** it became clear that one could not last long in a career even more ferocious than the legal profession.

So I asked, "How could a man like David not only survive, but thrive in that sort of workplace environment?"

The reply came: "David, as a boy, spent many cold and lonely nights alone with his sheep. It was then that he learned to hear my voice. You, my son, are not the first to have this sort of experience. There were countless nights when David found warmth and comfort in me and me alone. In that training period, David grew accustomed to the sound of my voice, just as his sheep had grown accustomed to his. He loved me and obeyed me.

He was successful because he learned to know my voice. When it came time for him to step into the place of a warrior, he was well prepared. When I told him, 'Turn now, David,' he would turn. When I instructed him to move, he would move. He knew there wasn't time for explanations. There was only time to trust. That is why David was a mighty man of valor, and that is what I want you to become as well."

Then God asked me to look around and tell Him what I was experiencing there in the cemetery.

I answered, "Peace and silence. Nothing but calm."

"That's right, my son," He said. "The battle is going to get fierce for you, and I want you to learn to fight with everything you've got. For when it is over, it is over, and you will rest in the peace that is yours and yours alone. You have only a small window of time in which to live. Live fully and richly and trust me as I guide you, and you will be successful. You will have no regrets."

I knew He was right.

HE'S GOD, FOR CRYING OUT LOUD.

There was much more to my day in Richmond—too much to tell. But He did allow me to work out at the gym at the end of the day. I thought I must have been making that part up, too, but He explained that in this journey of belief and obedience, there would be time to do the things I loved, as long as they didn't eclipse my love for Him.

I drove home in the blackness. The warm wind of the Indian summer ran its fingers through my hair as my mind sifted the random details of the day. In the last leg of the journey, tears streamed down my face as I thanked God for speaking to me the way He did that day.

His response only made the tears flow more freely. **"No, don't thank me. I've been waiting your whole life for this opportunity to speak with you."**

It was then that I realized what it must be like to have a son. There would be so many things you'd want to tell that child, so many questions you'd want to ask him. But it would be impossible until the inner workings of the ears were functioning and the mind had the ability to comprehend what it was hearing. Growth, development, and maturation would have to precede conversation. The only difference when it is our Father speaking to us is the additional element of belief. We have to really believe that He is willing and able to speak.

As I write this many years later, I am reminded of the intensity of the emotion I felt that September night. The tears that stream down my face now are just as real and just as fresh. I want to be saturated by God again, like I was that day. I want to listen, believe, and respond more in kind. I want to be more kind. I want fewer distractions; I want less of me and more of Him.

It can happen. I just have to ask, listen, and believe.

GLOBALWARNINGLOBALWARNINGLO

It's only fair to warn you that as you push into new places

with God and explore uncharted territory, you may experience strange reactions from your friends. You may even want to think twice before you share everything with everyone. That is a painful lesson I learned by trial and error. Many trials. Many errors.

Before he died (obviously), Rich Mullins, the singer-songwriter, drove several hours from Washington D. C., where he was doing a concert, to have dinner with me at a little bistro called **The Dumbwaiter.** We hadn't seen each other since the previous Christmas, when we had taken a road trip in his Jeep from Nashville to his family farm in Indiana.

Because Rich had such an incredible depth of understanding of God, and because he wrestled so intensely with his own humanity, I thought he might find my experience interesting. So over dinner I told Rich the story I've told here.

I waited in the silence for his response.

After what seemed like an eternity, Rich looked up and said, "I guess I would have thought Ezekiel was nuts, too."

CHECK, PLEASE.

It hurts to have a good friend and a sort of hero question your sanity. It stings when those you love begin to wonder if you may have gone too far on this adventure with an invisible God. I have to admit that my equilibrium was thrown off when Rich decided rather abruptly to end dinner. It wasn't long before he was in his Jeep heading back to D.C. and I was asking, *What kind of a fool am I? What kind of fool would believe that story, and what kind of fool would share it with Rich Mullins?* There were plenty of other things we could have talked about that didn't involve voices in my head.

AN A.D.D. MOMENT To secure a private boat in the Pirates of the Caribbean ride at Disneyland, pound your head while screaming the following as you take your seat. "Shut up, all of you, just shut up!"

I don't blame Rich for not believing. If he had been the one sharing that experience with me, I might have had the same response. But the more I thought about it, the more I realized just how important it was for me to tell that story. I decided then that I would much rather err on the side of belief than on the side of doubt. No matter how people respond to our stories at the moment, we might be planting a seed that will one day grow into something big.

Someone once said, "A man with an experience is never at the mercy of a man with an argument." But the real truth is that you don't need to argue with a nut. Just smile politely and leave quickly. And that is pretty much what Rich did. I felt like such a fool that night as I watched Rich's Jeep disappear into the blackness. His red taillights looked like signals warning against future tellings of this insane tale.

When it is all said and done, however, I don't know why I—
or anyone—should feel foolish for believing that God would speak to
us. After all, it is much harder to believe that He would come to earth
and die for us. How crazy is that?

What kind of fool believes?

Only a fool  FOR CHRIST'S SAKE.

AfterWords 2.5
THE SOUNDS OF SILENCE

TURNING OFF. TUNING IN.

AN AUDIOVISUAL FAST
AN AMAZING GOD FEAST

We are addicted to distraction. At every turn in every home, car, store, and plane, there are fifty million things to tune in, see, hear, watch, play, sing, or say. I am beginning to think that we are all insanely afraid of silence. What could possibly lurk in that dead air that would generate such a total scare?

Could there be a grand conspiracy to keep us from having enough silence—a big enough space into which God can speak? He may choose not to speak, but if we don't give Him the opportunity, we may miss the chance to hear the still, small voice of the one true God— the voice we need to learn to distinguish from among all the others, including our own. Sometimes it is necessary to turn off all of life's distractions so we can tune in to the voice of the one who made us.

BE STILL AND KNOW THAT
I AM GOD.

B<small>E STILL, BELIEVE, AND BE</small> C<small>OURAGEOUS.</small>

Could it be that the other team doesn't have to work all that hard anymore to lead us into temptation? We can hardly claim that the devil made us do it, when we can't even hear his enticing voice above the dizzying din.

HOW DO WE DO IT? WE BUY VOLUME, VOLUME, VOLUME!

I imagine it would be time-consuming to attempt to lead millions astray by whispering sweet nonsense into every heart of darkness. It's probably a lot more efficient to create machinery that makes enough noise and enough money to provide big screens, big screams, speaker towers, and subwoofers to keep the masses moving while the music makes hearts race and passions rage. The rhythms numb the mind and dull the senses. Lyrics linger longer and clog communication channels that should be cleared of clutter.

Movies, magazines, music, and television contain powerful images married to emotive music, which creates a sensory world of temptation that is more powerful than many lead us to believe. Who is leading us to believe? Why and where are we being led? Misled.

If our archenemy is bent on our destruction, and if he is the master of distraction, he is doing a great job. You've got to give credit where credit is due.

And do.

For God to enter the harsh reality of where we live and where we love—for us to hear God's voice and to see Him enter our domain— we must make the time and space for Him to reign. But that may be too close to home. That may be cutting way too close to the bone.

BUT WHAT PRICE PARADISE?

Jesus once told His friends that some of the things they would attempt, some of the supernatural things, could only be done with much prayer and fasting. Since I have low blood sugar, I'll stick to much prayer and feasting. That is the beauty of my 4:01 wake-up call. God knows all about us and what we are capable of doing. He showed me that morning that there are other forms of fasts.

For some of us, music is almost more important than food. I know I was getting fat on music, and even when it wasn't playing in my loft or car or office, it was playing in my head. How catchy those tunes are, and how amazing that I can effortlessly pull up songs complete with lyrics from fifteen years ago.

I don't care what you listen to, if it is filling your mind like so much bubble gum for the brain, it could only help to soak in a season of silence. That is what God called me to do. And that is what I did.

After my astounding road trip with God, I secluded myself from all of my friends and the usual sights and sounds of my life. For two solid weeks, I had dates with the God of the universe. It was the most fulfilling relationship I have ever known. After the first few days, when the strangeness wore off, I found myself falling in love with Him. I got intimately acquainted with the Father I had never really known and found a place of safety and warmth with Him that I hadn't realized could be my own. It's troubling to think that so many of us have never experienced this sort of intimacy with another human being, much less our Creator.

In that period of silence, I sat by the fire and listened as He spoke. I asked questions and basked in the beauty of who He is and the richness of His love. It was almost euphoric, and it was entirely addicting.

As my two-week audiovisual fast came to a close, I prepared to leave for Cannes, where I was to present a new television pilot. I decided that this fast was amazing and powerful and that I would continue it for the two weeks I was in France. The more I thought about it, the more I realized that I needed to hear God's voice more clearly on that trip than at any other time in my life. Like David before me, I was going to face a giant that was not friendly to those who wanted to set captives free.

My only weapon was a VHS copy of the trailer for a new program we were calling *(blah)³,* a new genre of programming for a young audience that spoke a global language while offering hope. I carried it in a small, hand-woven bag that I had slung over my shoulder. I had no TV sales savvy, no real resources, no contacts, and no elaborate display booth to draw in the international program buyers. I simply, and rather stupidly, walked the miles of corridors of the world's largest television exposition and randomly chose some of 14,000 participants to stop cold and ask, *"You wanna buy a watch?"*

It was even worse than I am describing. Many didn't speak English, and many who did pretended they didn't when I went into my spiel. I tried to convince complete strangers that they should somehow find a VCR in this monolithic place and spend their valuable time indulging a kook who couldn't even afford a booth. Not a single soul was interested in anything I had to offer. I felt like a fool.

At the end of the first dismal day at Cannes, I was exhausted and without a single lead. My feet felt like lead; my heart was even heavier. But the next morning, at an early hour that I now recognized as Godly, I received another wake-up call.

This time God suggested that we meet out on the balcony so that we wouldn't disturb the guy whose room I shared. I listened and obeyed. I walked out into the crisp autumn air and closed the door behind me. There, high above the French Riviera, God spoke.

"Tomorrow you are going as an ambassador of the Most High God," I heard Him tell me. "Today I wanted you to see what you are up against. But tomorrow you will go as my favored son—my ambassador. When you wake, I will tell you what to wear and what to take. Now, go back to bed."

I would have obeyed immediately, but I had locked myself out on the balcony—in my boxers.

WHEN GOD CHOOSES US FOR CERTAIN ASSIGNMENTS, HE HAS A FUNNY WAY OF REMINDING US WHO WEARS THE PANTS

God seems to choose to do extraordinary things through ordinary people if they are first willing to believe He is able to enter their present reality. The next step in the process is being willing to look foolish. I seem to excel in that arena.

I think that we are far more foolish far more frequently than we care to admit and that God enjoys watching us look a little foolish from time to time. Maybe He uses these times to remind us of who we are, who He is, and how miraculous it is that He can work with such frail beings to accomplish so much when we believe, trust, and obey.

This whole matter of foolishness is a test to see if we are willing to lose everything, including our pride and our reputation, for the sake of following Him with reckless abandon. After you begin losing things like that, you don't fear loss, because everything else pales in comparison.

IF YOU AREN'T LIVING ON THE EDGE, YOU'RE TAKING UP TOO MUCH SPACE

When I woke up on day two in Cannes, God told me to replace my torn jeans, T-shirt, and leather jacket with slightly more formal attire. He also asked me to carry a cigarette lighter. That seemed odd. But He's God. Although I was unclear on the reasons for these instructions, it didn't take long to find out.

After catching an early and costly taxi to the exposition center, I learned that my meeting with the heads of Times TV, India's largest and most prestigious media conglomerate, had been moved up a day. I wouldn't have had time to go back to the hotel, and my original choice of dress would have been offensive at best. "American confident casual" doesn't translate well into some cultures.

Ironically, the meeting was so successful and the men so moved by the program that they asked me to join them on the rooftop overlooking the spectacular seaside of southern France.

"This may seem inappropriate inasmuch as you are here selling a brilliant program," one of the top Times TV guys began. "But if you would drop this concept and move to India, we could make you a star in a country of 900 million people. We will find you a beautiful Indian cohost, and we can help make all your dreams come true."

I looked out across the shimmering water at the picturesque sailboats. My mind raced with the possibilities. I nearly fell for it. I almost forgot why I had come, not to mention the importance of the message of our show. (Pride comes before the fall, and when you are on the rooftop of the *Grand Palais,* a fall could do serious damage.) In the end, I came to my senses, remembered my mission and the power of the program, and left the rooftop to return to the chaotic exposition hall.

But the greatest part of day two was that God made good on His word. Everywhere I went, people stopped me to ask who I was and what I was doing at the event. Complete strangers took an interest in me, a nobody in the TV world trying to pitch a pilot. Those I stopped were receptive and genuinely interested in seeing the show, and many who watched were visibly moved. Some indicated a sincere interest in not only acquiring the series, but also in helping to develop it.

After several full and frenzied hours, I stopped at an espresso bar to refuel. Not thirty seconds later, an older, distinguished man with a thick Eastern European accent asked the barista for matches. He held a cigarette while the other fellow searched in vain. After what seemed like an eternity, the man became impatient in his thwarted quest for fire.

The lighter I carried began to burn a hole in my pocket.

"Here," I said, "I've got a lighter. Can I give you a light?"

He smiled and offered me a cigarette in exchange.

"No thanks," I replied. "I don't smoke."

He looked more than a little puzzled at my carrying a lighter in light of that revelation. I knew that I needed to talk with this man because we were targeting Eastern Europe, and I could tell he was a man of influence and power—mainly because of the way passing execs were treating him and because he kept blowing everyone off.

As he turned to leave, I desperately wanted to stop him. But I realized that if I were truly God's ambassador, protocol would dictate that *he* approach *me*. So I took my espresso to a nearby table and read over some notes. In a few minutes, I saw him looking my way. He walked toward me and, with genuine warmth, extended his hand and asked who I was and what I was doing at this event.

When I told him, his eyes lit up.

"I'm the head of Hungary's largest television network," he said.

I was guessing it was the *only* network, since Hungary had recently moved out of communist control.

"I have been looking all over for a new way to communicate with our young people," he continued. "Would you kindly send a copy of your show to my office in Budapest?"

My heart soared, and my confidence in the Creator reached an all-time high.

THE UN BEAT ABLE
LIGHTNESS OF BELIEVING

There is an unbelievably long list of faith-filled freedom fighters who moved when God chose to speak. Abraham left the land he loved for a mere promise. Moses, after chatting with some flaming foliage, faced the fury of Pharaoh to free his family—God's family. Joshua led the children of Israel across the Jordan into their promised inheritance, knowing the way although he had not gone that way before.

The common denominator is this: They all listened and believed. Most importantly, they all obeyed. The wackier God's command seems, the greater the obedience that is necessary and the greater the miracle that God can produce.

But the other side aspect of faith-fueled adventures is that sometimes after hearing God's voice, we decide how everything is going to play out. We jump to conclusions and make assumptions, many of which have nothing to do with what or why God originally spoke to us. After one or two mishaps, it is easy to begin to think these enterprises are crazy and to abandon this "hearing from God thing" altogether.

The program I was pitching at Cannes, although well received, was cancelled by the network that had commissioned its development. There had been a change of course, and of course, our dream was the first to go. I was devastated and confused, wondering

how God could have done so many powerful things, only to allow a
project with such potential die before it ever really lived.

My adventure in New Zealand was a bit like that as well. An
amazing program was birthed there, and it was nominated for a prestigious award in Switzerland, but I left the land down under nearly broke
and clearly confused as to why God had me go at all. The program was
never sold, and it was broadcast to only a tiny audience in New Zealand—
a Christmas gift to the people in the land of the long white cloud.

I can't tell you how much pain I have felt on the other side of
belief. Sometimes the confusion and questions seemed like almost more
than I could bear. But God may have had a much different outcome in
mind than the one I imagined. We are so very human, and our percep-
tions are limited and tweaked by our finite understanding and vision.

Besides, this journey called believe is a messy undertaking.
You will make mistakes. You must test the words your hear against His
authoritative Word because He never changes. His Truths remain the
same. Don't be disheartened when things don't work the way you
planned or like you thought God planned. He is infinitely creative, and
His timetable is often much different than our own. He does things in
ways you cannot imagine. God is always teaching, and every lesson
brings more life.

We may think that we are called to move mountains, when in
truth we are called only to be obedient. God has said that obedience is

better than sacrifice, so I guess that's His intent for our lives. No matter how messy it gets, or how disappointed you become, just hold on to the word that He has spoken. Do not let it go. Our responsibility is not to move the mountain—it is merely to believe and obey.

REMEMBER THE WORD TO YOUR SERVANT, UPON

WHICH YOU HAVE CAUSED ME TO HOPE. THIS IS

MY COMFORT IN MY AFFLICTION, FOR YOUR

WORD HAS GIVEN ME LIFE.

www.psalm@119.49–50.com/nkjv

THE SICKENING SOUNDS OF SILENCE

Hello darkness, my old friend. I wish someone would talk to me again.

Every mountaintop experience is followed by a slow, painful trek down. When I returned home from Cannes, I was met with a very real silence—a hauntingly hollow stillness that caused a sickening feeling in the core of my being. Due to my unexplained disappearance during my two-week AV fast, followed by my trip to France, my answering machine had grown strangely silent.

The hardest part was not the disappearance of my friends. That made sense. What I struggled with was the complete absence of the voice of God, the friend who had promised He would never leave or forsake me. The friend who would stick closer than a brother seemed nowhere to be found. I tried shouting Him out of hiding. Nothing. I thought I would play hard to get and maybe He would come back. (That ploy almost always worked in my other relationships.) Nothing. I tried ignoring Him and forgetting the month-long closeness we had just shared. But I was haunted by the memories in the middle of the silence.

I never dreamed I would miss God so much. Where was He when I needed Him most? I was completely alone. MY GOD, WHY HAVE YOU FORSAKEN ME?

This turn of events was totally unexpected and completely unnerving. I found myself in front of my fireplace one night shouting at God, asking Him to explain Himself if He ever felt like talking again.

THANK GOD FOR MERCY AND GRACE.

Thank God He does not react like I did, or I'd be dead by my own fury-filled judgment. Finally, out of the silence I heard a small voice that made its way through my madness.

"Take a walk along the canal with me," the voice said. "I want to explain something to you."

In the next few minutes, as I walked along the waterway that led to the sea, God began to speak.

"I AM THE GREAT GOD OF THE UNIVERSE.

I CHOOSE WHEN AND HOW I WILL SPEAK.

I WILL NOT BABBLE INCESSANTLY TO KEEP YOU HAPPY AND OCCUPIED.

I SPOKE OUT OF SILENCE TO TEACH YOU TO LISTEN.

NOW I HAVE USHERED THE SILENCE BACK IN TO TEACH YOU COMPASSION.

I WANT YOU TO REMEMBER, AND CONTINUE TO REMEMBER,

THE PAIN, THE EMPTINESS, AND THE LONELINESS MOST OF THE REST OF

THE WORLD IS FEELING AT ALL TIMES.

IN THAT PLACE OF REMEMBERING, YOU WILL FIND TRUE COMPASSION.

FOR I AM THE GREAT SOURCE OF HEALING, SALVATION, AND DELIVERANCE—

BUT WITHOUT COMPASSIONATE OUTLETS, WHAT GOOD IS MY SOURCE?"

G O D.

AfterWords 3.0

three in one and one in 3
god's own son
getting past the prodigal part.

I WILL SEND YOU THE PROPHET ELIJAH

BEFORE THAT GREAT AND DREADFUL

DAY OF THE LORD COMES.

HE WILL TURN THE HEARTS OF

THE FATHERS TO THEIR CHILDREN,

AND THE HEARTS OF THE CHILDREN

TO THEIR FATHERS; OR ELSE I WILL COME

AND STRIKE THE LAND WITH A CURSE.

www.malachi@4:5–6.com/niv

HEY KIDS,
I THINK WE'VE BEEN SMITTEN.

This is the pierced generation. Some of these piercings are readily visible to the eye; some are hidden and more painful. No, I'm not referring to areas concealed by clothing—I'm referring to a place much more guarded and tender. Before noses and navels were pierced, hearts were pierced, and not by choice. Often by someone else—someone who should have cared more.

The piercings we see are just reminders of the gaping hidden places that have been pierced and have not healed. Abandonment, abuse, neglect, and a litany of other offenses have left my generation pierced and in pain. No matter how much we apply alcohol or rotate the rings or clean the wounds, they are infected and festering. This infection keeps "us" from "them," and them from us, and all of us from our promised inheritance. So much pain. So little time.

Barring outside help, these wounds may never heal. We manage the madness by continuing to pierce the more obvious places in a desperate attempt to alert those around us to the pain that is hidden. What's a little more pain anyway?

ISN'TPAINBETTER THAN FEELING NOTHING AT ALL?

In the ancient world, a slave wore an earring as a sign that someone or something else controlled him. It was a covenant formed in blood. With the piercing of the flesh came the shedding of blood. After the piercing and the bloodshedding, the slave wore a ring to symbolize the covenant with the master.

Owned and maintained by the man.

The shedding of blood in covenant has a long tradition in our history. From the simple ceremony of blood brotherhood, with the cutting of the hand and the mingling of blood, to the more elaborate tribal rituals involving flesh hooks, bloodletting, ceremonial dances, chants, and prayers, shedding blood creates a bond with another human or an unseen entity.

We are shedding much blood today. Bullets pierce the flesh of young gang members who have entered into covenants or pacts with their packs—their brothers, their homeboys, their friends. Families are forged on streets of fear, and lives are inextricably linked in the jump-ins that spill so much precious blood and cost so many lives.

THIS IS A GENERATION ENSLAVED.

Jesus said that whoever commits sin is a slave to sin. Even though that may sound laughably foreign or old-fashioned, it doesn't take a rocket scientist to see the havoc that addictions create for all of us. There are ads in the *L.A. Weekly* offering help to those caught up in overeating, alcohol abuse, pornography, sexual massage, phone sex,

Internet chat rooms, prostitution, heroin addiction, smoking, compulsive gambling, and a lengthy list of other snares. What seemed so fresh and freeing now enslaves those who have walked blindly and blithely into the trap—whatever it is.

I'M PIERCED. Inside and out. I am no different from you or those you may fear. But it was the pain of my piercings that helped me write these words. I did not choose my first piercings. And those who did the piercing are undoubtedly unaware of the damage they have done. A piercing can be as simple as never hearing words of affirmation, or more complex, like emotional or spiritual abuse. For many of us, it doesn't really matter the brand or the color. Someone wounds us; a dark covenant forms in blood; and for many years we carry the weight of the sins of another. I, for one, was living out my desolate heritage, and my inheritance was death.

In our dizzyingly dysfunctional world, fraught with a father-less phenomenon, our land has surely been smitten. For many of us, the curse is bigger than we are. That missing father was not there to speak purpose and destiny into our lives, and we are now left wondering and wandering, trying desperately to make some sort of mark on a strip-mined, strip-malled landscape. It is frightening how low you can go when you are weighed down with invisible chains—chains that have been welded to the core of who you are or who you should have been or who you long to be.

If we come to believe that we can never escape, then we will prove true that self-fulfilling prophecy. We will die an unnecessary death—because one has already done that in our stead.

sOOEEEYYYYY... HERE PIGGY PIG PIG PIG.

The call of the wild. The wild child. The prodigal son of a proud progenitor—turned protector of the pigs. If you know this story, you probably remember that this same boy, the keeper of the pigs, was once an heir to a large and luxurious estate. But something went terribly wrong. He asked for his inheritance, then cast it down like powdered pearls before sweatless swine. This boy left his family to party like a pig, but he ended up living with them too. In the end, the pigs had the advantage. At least their meals were guaranteed. He had to steal when no one was looking.

A DECEPTION UNTO DEATH.

It could have been that Jesus told this story to show that reckless living leads to soulless loving and sordid lusting. Or perhaps His point was that some things that appear freeing are illusions to draw us in so deep that, when we finally discover the treacherous truth, we can't get out.

Both points are important parts of His story. But there's another moral that could actually seem immoral from a puritanically proper point of view.

This parable is so profound that I think we could be telling it wrong much of the time. We make it seem as if the prodigy-turned-prodigal—after having his senses assaulted by the sights, sounds, and mostly smells of assorted sins and sordid swine—at last came to his senses. But perhaps that is not what happened. It could be that the boy simply realized that he was getting the short end of the swill stick. While the pigs were living high on the hog, he was left high and dry, hungry and tired, and wanting very much to be home and safe and clean.

Wallowing in self-pity, this boy remembered that his father's servants had a lot better lot in life than he. The only thing keeping him a slave serving swill to swine was pure, high-octane vanity. So he swallowed his pride, turned tail, and headed for home. There might have been nothing unselfish or sincere about his change of course—at least nothing his father could endorse.

But it didn't matter. His father, a good father, spotted something more powerful and more important than model motives and real remorse. He saw the beginning of a real resurrection—a resurrection of his own flesh and blood, his beloved son, a grand foreshadowing of things to come. He recognized the gait, and his heart leapt into his throat as he ran recklessly toward the boy who once was dead, but now lived again.

Whatever they were, the boy's motives didn't stand a chance against his father's luxurious love. The old man didn't even hear the reasons that poured from the lips of his lad, because his shouts of joy drowned out everything the boy said or pretended to mean. This father did not see a filthy prodigal covered in the stuff of pigs. He saw his beautiful boy. This was flesh of his flesh and bone of his bone. This was the one he loved, and he had finally come home. That was all that mattered. Nothing else and nothing more.

Sometimes, however, there are unexpected surprises when we return home. The prodigal son may have expected his father's wrath, but I bet he was blindsided by the bitterness of the brother who had stayed at home. While the prodigal squandered the family's fortune, this boy had tried desperately to please his father. What he didn't realize was that he never had to work to earn his father's love—it was always there and always free. But when he saw his father lavish love on the prodigal, he boiled with hostility. Can you blame him?

Many of us are much worse than the prodigal boy or his bitter brother. If we haven't actually done the dirty deeds, we've thought a lot about them while going through the motions of trying to please our Father. We've envied those who live like the devil and dance with him too. We are either filthy from our faithless frolics on the dark side, or we are knee-deep in the stink of our own self-righteousness, arrogance, and pride. Both types of people are nauseatingly noxious in the nostrils of a Holy God.

As a rule, however, a prodigal is often more aware of his stench, so he seeks help to make himself clean. A bitter brother's self-righteous pride borders on the obscene. If you try to tell him, he won't know what you mean, and so he'll miss the beauty of who our Father is, what He freely gives, and what this freedom means.

> ARE YOU PLASTERED IN THE SQUALOR OF SWINE
>
> WHILE HAVING A RAUCOUS GOOD TIME,
>
> OR ARE YOU KNEE-DEEP IN SELF-RIGHTEOUS PRIDE,
>
> WHILE SECRETLY DYING INSIDE?

There is only one thing to do—only one thing you can do. Take a long, last look at your sty and make up your mind to leave. Decide to live in the fullness of the freedom for which you were formed. It requires only an acknowledgment of your stench and a desire to change. A desire to be changed. The Father is a good father who has not been cursing you in your absence. He is merely waiting with a broken heart for His lost child to come home—for you to come back, for the first or the fiftieth time.

The only thing that really matters is that we are willing to get up out of our swine-scene servitude and brush the mud off our pants while pointing ourselves toward home. A long walk before the dance.

This loving Father has been waiting patiently and passionately for you. He never gives up hope, no matter what we do. All that matters to our God is that the pig-plagued prodigal has turned his back on sin and is coming back again.

Back again.

In the near distance, you will see your Father running to meet you on that old, dusty road. It's a run He will make any time of any day or night, without judgment or spite. It is a run of redemption that none of us deserve. Yet over six billion are served—served by the Supreme God of the universe displayed on a sign of sacrificial love of a life well lived by the Son of the greatest Father of all.

If you are tired of running, He will run the last mile for you, with you, or to you. It all ends in a grand reunion of grace—a huge celebration feast—where God throws His strong arms around you and with kindness to spare, covers you with kisses and kills you with compassion.

FEAR NOT, FOR I HAVE REDEEMED YOU;
I HAVE CALLED YOU BY YOUR NAME; YOU ARE MINE.
WHEN YOU PASS THROUGH THE WATERS,
I WILL BE WITH YOU;
AND THROUGH THE RIVERS,
THEY SHALL NOT OVERFLOW YOU.

WHEN YOU WALK THROUGH FIRE, YOU SHALL
NOT BE BURNED...
FOR I AM THE LORD YOUR GOD,
THE HOLY ONE OF ISRAEL, YOUR SAVIOR...
BRING MY SONS FROM AFAR, AND MY DAUGHTERS
FROM THE ENDS OF THE EARTH—EVERYONE WHO IS
CALLED BY MY NAME, WHOM I HAVE CREATED FOR MY
GLORY...THAT YOU MAY KNOW AND BELIEVE ME,
AND UNDERSTAND THAT I AM HE.
BEFORE ME THERE WAS NO GOD FORMED,
NOR SHALL THERE BE AFTER ME.

www.isaiah@43.1–10.com/nkj

MY GOD, WHAT HAVE I DONE?

It really doesn't matter. It's not about what you have done;
it's what He has done and what that means to you. His love covers a
multitude of sins. His life lived through you will bring you peace and

redemption in the end. Not many of us can relate to that kind of crazy love. None of us have earned it, and we do not deserve it. It is a gift for the taking for those who believe it.

This is the Father we've missed, the Father we've seldom known—the great God who is so often misrepresented, misinterpreted, misquoted, mistaken, and misty-eyed. Our God cries.

He does, you know.

This tenderhearted Father is not concerned by our present state. He doesn't smell the foul of the waste or the things we've embraced. He looks past the bruises, the scars, scabs, and tears. He knows the end from the beginning, and he understands all our fears.

A HEART THAT IS MENDED.
A SON NOW BEFRIENDED.

But there are more than hugs and kisses in this grand reunion. This father, **the** father that Jesus described in His vivid portrayal, was and is His Father. Your Father. And mine. This loving dad, unafraid of the sight and smell of his beloved son, does not order him to get cleaned up before He welcomes him in.

Instead, He wraps his robe of righteousness around the filthy but beloved boy, covering his sins in the covenant of the blood, shed by the one who was pure and the one who was true. The I Am that I Am, the everlasting, the friend, the beginning and end. All we need to do is ask, then turn our backs on what was and our faces toward what will be.

> AND BECAUSE YOU ARE SONS,
> GOD HAS SENT FORTH THE SPIRIT
> OF HIS SON INTO YOUR HEARTS,
> CRYING OUT, "ABBA, FATHER!"
> THEREFORE YOU ARE NO LONGER
> A SLAVE BUT A SON, AND IF A SON,
> THEN AN HEIR OF GOD
> THROUGH CHRIST.

www.galatians@4.6–7.com/nkj

The stench of the prodigal son is now covered by a robe of righteousness. A ring of eternal covenant is on his finger instead of through his pierced ear.

There is no longer a reason to shed blood. The perfect blood of the perfect Son has already been shed in our stead. It covers the multitudes mired in sickening sin. It covers this pierced boy and the prodigal and his brother in the parable that Jesus told. This boy was not to be a slave—he was and is a son and will forever be. And He whom the son sets free is **free.** Not in word only, but also in **deed.**

GOD'S SON WAS PIERCED

The perfect Son was pierced inside and out. For you and for

me. His outer piercings are there to point to the inner piercing—the heart that aches for all of our pain, for all our tears. His pierced hands and feet are an outward sign, a proclamation and a testament of His love for all mankind—all types, all kinds. They are reminders etched on His palms and on His feet so we will never forget. No matter where He walks or whom He touches, everyone will see the mark that He left for you. For me.

FOR FREE.

Make your way down the road to the Father you feared. Find the courage and the strength to kiss your pride, prostitutes, and pigs good-bye. Forget the B. A., the B. S., and the Ph.D.—the IOUs and the CODs. Just decide to make your way back and ask, no matter what it may appear to cost in terms of your pride. Before you know it, you will find yourself wrapped in the warmth and strength of the love of the Father's arms. Your Father's arms. You will find yourself lost in the fullness of who He is and who He has called you to be.

You are His beloved child. You are what brings Him joy, and you are exactly who He created you to be. The rest is lived out in the loving and the learning—and in setting other captives free.

He whom the Son sets free is free. **Indeed.**

B   E   L   I   E   V   E   .

PARTY ON, PRODIGAL PEOPLE.

Party with pigs and prostitutes and you pick up some nasty viruses. We don't talk much about sin in the chat rooms of our on-line culture. We are far too civilized to be burdened by an archaic attribution that brings us shame. But sin is sin by any other name. I just learned that the Hebrew word *sinner* means "one who has lost his way." When we lose our way and step out of the perfect order—the system set in motion by one much higher than us—we'll pick up viruses that will corrupt and fragment our hard drives and our hard lives. It is tough enough to make it through life without the added chaos that comes with corruption.

Sin is all around us. Everywhere I look, I'm tempted by something or someone promising to bring me everything I think I want or need. In reality, what I need, I already have. There is just some serious downtime while my system loads the softwhere and works the bugs out of my operating system. Often it takes much longer than we expect, so we start looking for other ways to mend what has taken many years to break. Corruption comes when we think we can circumvent the path that promises life, because, honestly, none of us is very patient. And few of us truly trust that God has our highest good in mind. We limit Him when we think He is limiting us.

BEING CONFIDENT OF THIS VERY THING.... HE WHO HAS BEGUN A GOOD THING IN YOU WILL COMPLETE IT. PERIOD.

I don't care who you are, you do it. You—we—limit God. It is human nature, and it corrupts our system, preventing us from fully moving into the place where we can make a difference in a world that desperately needs one.

WHAT ARE WE FRETTING FOR?

Whether we are caught up in big sins—the ones the high and mighty point out from atop their watchtowers—or tiny ones that we keep hidden away as we rationalize them, we are all plagued by nasty viruses. If researcher George Barna's findings are correct, those who claim to believe in Christ live no differently than those who do not. That means there really is no distinction between us and them. We have become just like them, even though we point our dirty little fingers at their dirty little deeds. As a result, no one is free.

So what happened to the prodigal who finally came home? What happens when *we* finally come home? In Jesus' telling, the Father threw a giant rave in honor of his beloved boy. He filleted the fatted calf, raided the wine cellar, and invited everyone he knew to come and see that his son lived and the Father loved, no matter what contaminated water had passed under their bridge. I guess they lived happily ever after.

GUESS AGAIN.

Life is never as simple or antiseptic as depicted in fables, parables, and fairy tales. What Jesus didn't say here—although He did in other places—is that even though a beautiful robe now covers the smell of swine and cheap red wine, there are consequences to our actions: diseases attached to our decisions, problems packed onto our perversions, and chains clamped to our addictions. There is no magic wand to wave to make everything we loathe disappear. It is usually much more painful and difficult than that, and it is worse for those around us who are trying to help us get free. Although we've grown accustomed to the smell, it is powerfully pungent to everyone else.

CLEANING UP AFTER THE PARTY.

Many of us struggle after living fast and loose with prostitutes and pigs. When the party is finally over, and we find ourselves home and alone, there are those dark times when our self-esteem sinks lower than low and there is nowhere to go—except back to what we know. We do it because it's easy, and if memory serves, we can dull the pain, forget the chains, and for just a few minutes or hours be free—free to remain addicted and in bondage until we are finally ready to believe.

If you *think* the journey of believe sounds hard, tedious, and boring, just wait till you actually try walking it. It can be even worse than that—at first. Just like the subterfuge of sin, there is a deceptive light cast on living free. If you have ever tried to take up weight lifting, running, snowboarding, or any activity that requires discipline, endurance, or fitness, you know how awful the early days are before the glory days come.

For a long time, I admired the snowboard culture. Even the clothes looked so cool. Despite the fact that I had been a downhill skier since I was knee-high to a snake's belly and sneered at "boarders" who seemed to do more sitting than sliding, I finally caved. I bought a board and all the gear and hit the mountains—with my face, mostly. Over and over, snow packed up my nose and in my ears. My expensive glasses broke, and I learned that, with very little trouble at all, swearing could be my second language. But those boarders appeared so carefree and fluid in the videos. Why did this sport feel no different than head-butting busses?

By the end of the first day, my end was frozen, bruised, and nearly broken. My face resembled that on which I sit. But for some crazy reason, I decided to try it all again. No one paid me—I had to pay. A lot. After the second day, there were a few isolated moments when I thought that I looked like the guys I admired. (I have a vivid imagination.) I felt confident and cocky for a few short seconds before I taste-tested the man-made snow—several million shameful times in a row.

Snowboarding is now my favorite sport. I look forward to packing my rig the night before the trip, and I can barely sleep those couple of hours before the alarm rips apart the predawn darkness. I still remember the pain of the early days. But it was all worth it. First, I had to see something I admired, and then I needed to believe I could do it. I did, and I do.

Life is a lot like that. The only problem is that we don't have many models worth admiring and emulating. We have excessive examples of how not to live and why that seems to pay. But when you look carefully, **behind the sins,** you realize we are not being told the whole story—just as Jesus didn't tell the whole story of the prodigal and what it could mean for our new lives as sons.

All of us have to come to realize that this new way of living, back at home with the Father, is going to take some serious adjustments. It will seem that our freedom has been co-opted and that everything that comes naturally is actually not the natural way to live.

PAINFUL DAYS PRECEDE LIVING FREE.

Part of the pain involves sweating out addictions and bad habits. Some nights you may find yourself scrambling to find your phone book so you can dial up someone or something to help you ease the pain. But that is far too easy and not at all free. The price may seem reasonable at the moment, but you'll be billed $3.99 a minute for a long time after the high has turned to an incredible low.

In the middle of this madness, the lie comes to say, "You've slipped again. Now there is nowhere left to go but back to what you used to know." The beauty of the rest of the story is this: The forgiveness that came so freely on the road home—from a father so filled with joy—is the same for us at all hours of the night, every night till the end of time. We just have to lose our pride and that nagging voice that whispers the lie. There is nothing that will separate you from the love of God that is in Christ Jesus.

NOTHING.

No matter what you do, or how many times you do it, nothing will separate you. Except you.

DO NOT BELIEVE THE LIE

You have the choice to believe. If you believe that the God of the universe is bigger than your problems, your addictions, and your many stuttered steps, then you will continue to get up out of the pigsty of your mind. You will rinse off the mud and the dung, and you will continue the journey that you have begun. That is all that is required of you. God will take care of the rest. And the rest.

FOR IT IS GOD WHO WORKS IN YOU—
BOTH TO WANT TO DO AND TO DO WHAT IS
RIGHT. THIS WAY YOU WILL BE BLAMELESS AND
HARMLESS AS CHILDREN OF GOD WITHOUT FAULT
IN THE MIDDLE OF A CROOKED AND PERVERSE
GENERATION—AND YOU, WITH THE POWER THAT
COMES FROM YOUR COVENANT IN BLOOD,
WILL SHINE AS LIGHTS IN THIS
DARK AND CROOKED PLACE.

www.philippians@2.13–15.com.

The next step is coming to a place where you believe beyond what you see. So many times I look in the mirror and see such a destroyed and tired sinner. But my mirror and my eyes are flawed—severely flawed—so I am asking for the ability to really see. Ask God to open the eyes of your understanding to see beyond what is and into the way things ought to be.

SEEING IS BELIEVING.
(IF YOU'RE LIMITED THAT WAY.)
BELIEVING, YOU SEE,
IS LIVING,

SO THAT WHAT'S APPARENT
DOES NOT GET IN THE WAY.

Remember, it is all about asking. In order for me to believe that I am going to make it to the end and become who He intends, I must see past the here and now into the there and then. I need first to believe. And then I will see. But before all of this is possible, hope must precede.

STAND FAST STAND FIRM.
AND WHEN YOU HAVE DONE
EVERYTHING ELSE,
SHUT UP AND STAND.
AND BELIEVE.

The trickiest part of all this is maintaining a willingness to believe beyond what you can see or what you think you see. No matter what, there will be voices that remind you of what was and how easy it all seemed.

It was easy to not snowboard. It was a pain to learn. And now that I'm getting better, I'm loving life more every season. But the point is, I had to first believe. I had to want to believe, and I had to see something worth believing. **Believe, and then you'll see.**

"I WOULD BE A CHRISTIAN IF IT WEREN'T FOR THE CHRISTIANS."

GHANDI. (YOU. ME.)

If you are at all like me, you have very few examples of Christians you would want to imitate. Most Christians don't live the way they should or say they do. But guess what? Neither will you. So take your eyes off them—and it wouldn't hurt to take your eyes off yourself too. Instead, set your sights on the one for whom your faith is named. Use Him as your example, and extend the same grace you have received to those you find wanting. They, like you, need more of Him—more grace, more strength, and more belief.

JESUS, PROTECT ME FROM YOUR FOLLOWERS.
A GREAT BUMPER STICKER

The good news is that God is not as concerned with the end as He is with the means. He is overseeing the process that produces the product. He knows the end from the beginning, so He isn't holding His breath wondering how it is all going to turn out—how *you* are going to turn out. He wants to see you living it and meaning it and risking it and loving it—and loving *them,* no matter how offensive they may be.

We are, too. But we're closer now to who we were meant to be.

But there is more to the story than just belief. There is a power source that is rich and ready for the taking. Because you are a son, you are free to tap into that source whenever and however and as often as you like or need. That is possible because of shared blood—the blood that is yours because you are a son.

BOUND BY BLOOD.

There is more to blood than just the covenant. Blood is what makes a son a son. It is the blood covenant that enables you and me to walk into freedom and claim our inheritance. There is authority that comes with the blood, and it enables us to rise out of our makeshift maturity to make sure that we claim a life that is authentic and real. No matter how things look or how we feel.

As crazy as this may sound, you hold the key to your own freedom. When you step into your role as a son, you will have the authority to exercise your rights as an heir to one incredible estate. There is power as a son, because there's **power in the blood. Use it.**

VIRUS CHECK

It is important for us to do a daily virus check to find out if we have exposed ourselves to cookies or downloads or tainted e-mail that may have corrupted our system. Start now. When that which *was* seems to be playing louder than that which *is to be,* you have to use your authority to break the habits, patterns, and mind-sets that imprison you. Speak out and take charge of your situation. Speak out with the authority that is vested in you as a son and an heir.

You are not to be pushed around and bullied any longer.

(But you will be until you start to believe and live like you mean it.)

How many times do we find ourselves in the same stupid, destructive activity over and over again no matter how many times we ask God to do something about it? Guess what, kids, He already has. And if we are smart, we will open our eyes and use the tools and weapons He has given us.

WHOEVER IS A SON OF GOD DOES NOT SIN,

FOR HIS SEED REMAINS IN HIM;

AND HE CANNOT SIN,

BECAUSE HE HAS BEEN BORN OF GOD.

www.1john@3.9.com/nkjv

I have a problem with that. I now know that I'm a son, yet I am awfully good at sinning. Continually. Habitually. Ridiculously. What am I supposed to do with that nice sentiment when it doesn't seem to apply to someone as screwed up as me? That was my question, and it's one all of us should ask if we are truly being honest. I have recently learned what we are supposed to do with that passage: believe it and use it.

Every time God's Son was faced with a temptation, He simply quoted the truth back to the tempter. It was effective, and I'm guessing it still is. Every time Jesus was weak, tired, and hungry, guess who would appear with an offer He just "couldn't refuse"? But Jesus never entertained the idea; He simply used His authority *as a son* to invoke the power that was and is resident in His Father's words.

When something seductively vile is staring us in the face, we should use those same words as our first shield of defense: "I'm sorry, I cannot do this (insert heinous-yet-oh-so-tempting activity here) because I am truly a son of the Most High God. His seed, His blood, is in me, and now that I am one with Him, I cannot do that which He cannot do." Sorry. Thanks for playing.

Other passages work as shields as well, and there is great power in the Word. Speak the Word; believe the Word; and use it for your protection and safety and covering and defense. Rest in the fact that those words are not your words and that as a son you can claim the power that resides in them. God set our entire existence into motion from mere words. He brought worlds into being by simply speaking. Words. We need to use His words to bring our world in line with the truth of who we are when we become one with Him.

CASTING DOWN ARGUMENTS
AND EVERY HIGH THING THAT EXALTS ITSELF
AGAINST THE KNOWLEDGE OF GOD,
BRINGING EVERY THOUGHT INTO CAPTIVITY
BY THE OBEDIENCE OF CHRIST.

www.2corinthians:@10.5.com/nkjv

SPELL CHECK. Keep in mind that this is not a mantra or spell. These words are potent because the Author of all has filled them with power. If we are under that authority, in the proper place of being a son, then we have access to that same power. The only trick involved is to believe.

Once the corrupting factors and viruses are eradicated from our hard drives, we will be free to move in the might and power necessary to make a lasting difference in our world. I don't know about you, but I'm tired of being powerless over that which I have been promised power. I guess we just needed to know the truth and how to use it, and then put it all into practice.

Finally, being a good son takes some serious time, especially if there has been damage done in the formative years. If you haven't guessed it by now, I'm about as prodigal as you can get. I believe it all started when I was young and my parents split up. Although I had an amazing stepfather, I never really had what every kid should have: a strong bond with a dad—one that is formed through millions of moments spent together over the course of a lifetime. There is no substitute for that.

I will never forget my first breakfast alone with my dad. It was the day after Christmas just a few years ago. I had visited him many times, but he always seemed to be gone in the mornings, so I usually ate breakfast with his wife, my stepmother, Jan. But this time was different. That year he and I were left alone among the empty boxes and torn-up wrapping paper.

Sitting down at the table, with the Christmas tree twinkling in a stupid Jiminy Cricket kind of pattern behind us, my dad asked, "So, what kind of cereal do you like?"

It felt so odd. He wasn't asking if I would prefer Frosted Flakes or Raisin Bran—he really had no idea what kind of cereal I liked. In that moment, I realized we didn't know a heck of a lot about each other. And it didn't help to wish upon a star. What should have been now seemed too far. When I got past that painful realization, I found myself in a complete panic, wondering what on earth a son was supposed to talk about with a dad over Cheerios.

This may sound minor. But minor things become major problems years down the road. I didn't have an inkling of what I had been missing with my father until it was too late. I can't blame anyone. I don't need to. The damage was done, and that frightening breakfast spurred me to get out of the house as fast as I could to regroup and think. I was angry, torn up, and confused.

CHEERIO, DADDY-O

On my high-speed drive away from the father I wanted desperately to know, questions kept racing through my mind. What do you say to your dad at breakfast when it feels like you are eating with a complete stranger? Probably the same things you say to anyone at breakfast. The only problem was that I panicked, and I couldn't have felt "stranger." It's ironic. I once worked on a live television show where I entertained guests like Charlton Heston on a regular basis, and I never had trouble coming up with clever things to say to guys who part the Red Sea on the big screen. But when it came to my playing the part of son to my father, I encountered serious stage fright.

EXIT STAGE RIGHT

Now, a few years later, as I observe the rest of the world, I witness incredible little moments that give me insight into what relationships between dads and their children are like. The other day at the car wash, I noticed a great big kid sitting on his dad's lap while they waited for the guys to finish drying their van. Nothing was being said, and the dad was gently stroking his son's back. Both were staring at their family car. Neither seemed worried about what to say—they just soaked up each other's love in silence.

A few months ago, while staying on a ranch with some friends in Oregon, I watched a busy, tired dad drop all his cares and concerns to lovingly listen to his daughter as we drove home in their old black truck. She was not required to be witty or profound. All that mattered was that they were together, and the rest of the world just melted away for the duration of that drive. She had the love of her daddy, and for now she had his ear. He was with his daughter, and her words were what he loved to hear. I think this ride was the beginning of my journey back home. Even though I sometimes roam.

ROAMING CHARGE$ APPLY

I'm not panicked about all of this anymore. I just needed some time to process this father-son stuff, and I will undoubtedly need more. But I've come to some powerful conclusions. I missed out on those amazing bonding times that can never be replaced. I will never be able to share 38,000 bowls of cereal with my dad, nor will I be able to see him sitting in the stands at my Little League games or at another painful grammar school musical. We're both too old for that. You can never go back.

But what I can do is ask my Father, my God, to make some sort of amazing arrangements that will enable something supernatural to happen—something bigger than the pain we share. Something that will begin to fill a father-son void and start the process that will turn my heart to my father and the heart of my father to me so that we will no longer be smitten by the curse. And both of us will be free.

I want to learn to become a son, and I want to know how to relate to my dad. I want to call him Dad and know what that means. I want to love him recklessly and completely, and I want to know him just as well. But I think that will all take time. And the will to believe.

We've got to be patient with ourselves in areas like this. Not just in becoming sons to our biological fathers, but also in becoming sons and daughters to God our Father. We are all just fumbling our way toward ecstasy, and it can only serve our purposes to be kind to one another as we test a newfound role of son, daughter, mom, or dad.

Our Father has infinite patience with us, and I'm guessing He hopes we can be patient with ourselves. A good father doesn't get angry with his child for not being able to walk after the first round of lessons. He is there for every painful fall, and he is there to help get the toddler back on his feet with encouragement to try again. And again. This is a long journey, and there are many pitfalls on the way. We need a good dad to watch our backs—to stroke our backs and to love us back—till we get to the place our God intended us to be.

Home and safe and clean.

Remember, you don't have to do all the work. You just have to want to have the work done in you and through you. He who has started a good thing is faithful to complete it.

BE FAITHFUL TO BELIEVE IT.

IF THE SON MAKES YOU FREE, YOU SHALL BE FREE INDEED.

www. john@8.36.com/nkjv

AfterWoRDs 4.5
DEATH AND THE WILL
LETTING GO OF YOURS. ACCEPTING HIS.

THE PROMISED INHERITANCE.

WEBSTERS UNIVERSAL UNABRIDGED, 1943

Will, n. [ME. Wille, from AS. Willa, will.]

> 1. That faculty or power of the mind by which we determine either to do or not to do something which we conceive to be in our power; the power of control which the mind possesses over its own operations. That which is strongly wished or desired.

> 7. In law, the legal declaration of a man's intentions as to what he wills to be performed after his death.

WILL YOU BELIEVE? It is one thing to want to believe, and it is quite another to actually do it. It is almost like that stupid little story that goes something like this: **I can say I believe you are able to push a wheelbarrow on a high-wire over Niagara Falls. But if I *really* believed, I would have to get in it.** That is what this interactive journey with God is all about. He is asking us to get into His wheelbarrow and trust that He can do what He says. But the truly frightening part of this act of faith is that it's not just *once* over Niagara Falls. This trip in a one-wheeled bucket goes on and on and on, over all the things we fear, the things we hide, and the things we love. This journey of belief involves a complete and total surrender of our will so that another, much higher will can take us from one shore to the other. Safely and in one piece.

AND IN ONE PEACE.

All of this goes against our American dream. This is the land of the individual—the few, the proud, the unredeemed. But the me-first mindset doesn't just pervade the land of the free and the home of the brave; cultures worldwide celebrate self. Magazines, movies, television, and books are manuals of self-centered, self-serving destruction. It is a foreign and frightening thought to live for the sake, and under the will, of another. I want what I want, and I want God to sanction it—period. If not, I'll just find a more convenient god—one that gets it and gets me and my needs. There are an awful lot of gods out there. I'm sure one or a mix of many will line up with my reverse theology.

PICK A GOD, ANY GOD, BUT DON'T LET ME SEE IT— LEAD TO MY INCONVENIENCE.

Well, if you really want to believe in the one true God who made you and all that you see, it doesn't exactly work the way you would like. Believing involves the will—that decision-making ability all of us have that propels us into careers and car payments, marriages and mortgages, lifestyles and colleges. For many of us, this will is made of steel. It is unyielding, unbreakable, and mostly unbendable. The iron bars of our will keep us locked in places we don't really enjoy. But the thought of letting go and letting another take charge is more difficult than even our self-destructive endeavors.

In order to benefit from a will—as in last will and testament—there first must be a death. In order for us to benefit from the will of another, the will of one so much higher, death must come—to us and to our will.

Are we willing to let go of what we love the most, including our lives, in order to love the one we *should* love the most at any price? Do we truly believe? Are we willing to die so others might be set free?

Since we are all called to be freedom fighters, I like to look at the lives of those who have gone before. William Wallace and Moses both had to learn to let go before they could realize the fullness of their purpose in life.

William Wallace, as portrayed in the movie *Braveheart,* had to lose his one true love at the brutal hands of his English enemy before his resolve kicked in. Until then, he wasn't ready to lay it all down. Her death ignited his will and set him on fire for his people's freedom. The needs of the many took precedence over the will of the one. I admire William Wallace for placing his life on the line so his brothers and sisters could be free. He didn't get to see what his blood bought, but his death changed the will of the people, who saw how he lived and that he died for what he truly **believed.**

Moses, like William Wallace, was a freedom fighter before freedom fighting was cool. You could safely say that Moses was very "old school." His will died many deaths so the will of the one who made him could be accomplished in his lifetime and beyond.

This was a man of rare privilege. Raised as a son in the house of Pharaoh, he lived in the lap of luxury while his people, God's people, died in the throes of slavery, dropping like flies in the heat of the Egyptian sun.

Why would Moses choose to leave his life of royalty, leisure, and security to stand against a system that enslaved—to put his life on the line for the people he would save? It's especially odd when you consider that the people weren't even sure they wanted to be saved. Why take a risk like that? Whatever for? Was he bored?

Moses faced death as he moved into the will of the one who made him. Sometimes it is the death of another that gets us started on our journey. Moses killed an Egyptian, and because gossip is like an addiction, the word spread. His unredeemed act took him (quickly) out of the company of the king, to the backside of the desert, and into the company of fleas. Sin can do that. But God is bigger than our impetuous natures and our vile misdeeds—murder and every brand of perversion—even pompous piety.

Moses was in the desert when he began to truly believe. Maybe he had no choice. Whatever the case, it was a dry time that brought Moses to a place where he could hear God's voice. Then he was willing to listen and believe. After the death of the Egyptian, the death of his earthly inheritance, and the death of his dreams, it was time to read the will—the will of the one who speaks in the most unlikely ways and uses us despite our brokenness and depravity. But it was first death, then life—real life for Moses, the Hebrew children, and even some of the adults.

It is no different for us. The story of Moses merely foreshadows the many deaths that we all must face—death to who we think we are, death to our dreams, and death to all those things that keep us farther from living free.

As a kid, I was fascinated by the world of fashion, film, and frivolity. I wanted nothing more than to make my mark in some significant way, so the world would remember that I had been here and that I was fabulous. Well, God had another plan. He did place creative gifts within me, and those gifts were meant to be used, not ignored, and definitely not abused. He gives all of us dreams, gifts, and abilities, and He also gives us free will to choose how and where those gifts will be used.

But first He wants us to allow death to come to all of those things so He can breathe life back into them—for another resurrection of yet another beloved son. Often, God is a God of symmetry. He is clever and creative, and it seems that all He does has a greater, higher, or more complex purpose—a purpose deeper and richer than what is readily apparent.

I DIE SO HE CAN LIVE IN ME.

I moved to the West Coast to pursue my dreams, and in time I started doing some of the things I had longed to do. I wrote advertising copy, designed clothing, and occasionally did some acting. But even as I began to realize my dreams, there was something empty about it all. As I looked around at those I admired, I found that their lives rang hollow, even more so than mine, despite the fact that they had "arrived." It became clear that the hollowness would not disappear when I finally made it to the land of my dreams.

That's when I really started communicating with God. There in Seattle, on a rainy and depressing day, I looked up toward the heavens and, more out of disbelief than belief, asked the most important question anyone can ask:

God, are You real?

P.S.: "If you are real, you are going to have to show me. If you are real, I will give you my life and you can do with it whatever you please. (major cringe here) If you are not real, then I am going to be the best hedonist I can possibly be." (devilish grin here)

In truth, I was hoping for the latter rather than the former. Hedonism came far more naturally to me. Obedience and sacrifice felt about as good as sliding naked down a banister of razorblades into a vat of iodine. But I think I must have meant that prayer—or whatever it was. It was laced with anger, confusion, and angst, but there was someone more caring and loving than I listening at the other end of that random request. Thank God.

Rather than drag you into my private hell, suffice it to say that over the next several weeks and months, God did amazing things to prove that He is real. He will, you know, if you ask. God knows how much I had disliked church people in suits and ties and perma-smiles, so He sent a very peculiar collection of misfit believers my way to confirm my fear that He was indeed real. People I used to dance with in clubs came out of the woodwork to tell me about this incredible God they had fallen in love with. These were people I had watched fall in love with a lot of other people on a regular basis—so I got to see them wrestle with their humanity as they wrestled with God and His amazing grace.

I was astounded at the extraordinary display God used to show me that He was not only real, but that He cared enough to send people I would listen to instead of those I had learned to fear. He knew I had a long way to go (and still do) before I will wear a suit and perma-smile, but I have to learn to love the ones who do. God forgive them...and me...and you.

This journey, like all journeys, involved death after death to my dreams. It still does. But as I watch His incredible plan unfold in my life, along with His new and improved dreams, I am learning to trust my Father. One of these days I may be able to climb into His little wheelbarrow as He does His wild high-wire dance over those raging waterfalls.

TRUST.

That's what this thing is all about. It is becoming again like a little child who is content to be with his dad as they walk through the crowded streets or a busy mall. The boy simply holds onto His father's big finger while contentment plasters itself all over his face—or at least where the sucker stuff isn't. That boy and this boy know somewhere deep inside that everything is all going to turn out great—despite the crazy things and strange people all around them—because his daddy is leading the way.

Forget the wheelbarrow—I want to walk this thing out with my Father. Just give me a hand to hold and a sucker or two, and we will be on our way. I find that a little sugar on a regular basis is good for the soul—trust me on this one thing.

TRUST YOUR FATHER ON ALL THE REST.
AND THEN REST.

AFTERWORDS 5.0
LOGGING ON

ACCESSING HIS HOME PAGE–HIS WILL.

YOU KNOW, JESUS, YOU REALLY BLEW IT.

You said the right things, believed the right things, but you just didn't have the right handlers. Truth is, you didn't manage your PR well, and your publicity machine was virtually nonexistent. The miracles were great, but you should have worked the press. Why did you tell those wretched slobs to keep quiet? I don't get it, Jesus. You don't have a clue, do you? You ended up with a pretty bad rap in the end—condemned by your converts and betrayed by your friends. It's sad, really. Not a soul at your side when it all came to an end.

For a guy claiming to be God, you have a lot to learn. You could've done a whole lot more with your scam if I had been around to help. You know what I think your biggest problem was? Timing, baby. Timing. And your presentation was lacking, to say the least.

I would've ditched the birth in the barn thing. It's quaint, I'll give you that much, but it doesn't play well with the power brokers on

Wall Street or in Washington or Hollywood. If it was understatement you were after, I think you shot too low. The poor bought your humble thing in a big way. The wealthy E.vangelists capitalized on that and roped in those poor suckers. Now the whole thing has my head spinning and the telethon phones ringing.

You don't look well, Jesus. You need some time at the beach. I can hook you up with a place. Great views, good food. Remind me.

But truthfully, apart from a few major errors, I like your style. You might be on to something—you just needed to manage things a little better. Like when you were born. CNN coverage on that whole virgin thing could've worked. The tabloids would've eaten out of your hands. Nobody would've bought it, mind you, but they would've bought *you,* and the international press could've pushed your career a lot farther, a lot faster.

What were you thinking with that whole "lets not launch my career until I'm thirty" business? Why not take advantage of the beauty of your youth to do some modeling or acting? You could've gone out in style and died in a *Boxster*—the media loves that sort of thing. If you'd checked out in a sleek Porsche at your peak, your mug would've been on posters, postcards, and calendars. *A Rebel without A Cross.* Hey, I kinda like that. I'll bill you for that one.

You could've formed a pretty serious band with that rag-tag group you hung out with. You would've been a superstar, Jesus Christ,

I really believe.

WHAT'S THE BUZZ? TELL ME WHAT'S A HAPPENING, WHAT'S THE BUZZ?

Well, it's all over now, and there's not much you can do about it. We could work on some sort of revival thing—you know, bring you back for a second-coming kind of tour. See if talk around town about you and your antics might pick up again, sort of like what happened for Franky before he checked out. Maybe we could do some kind of duet CD with some really big names to put you back in the spotlight. You know, if you changed your tune a little bit, lightened up your act—let go of that death lingo, let's say—I might be able to get you on Letterman midweek, or maybe even Leno.

We've got work to do, you and me. Serious work. But I think you're a player. And if we play our cards right, I can make you a hot property all over again. Bigger than you were in the day. Bigger than even the Beatles, say.

WHO IN THE WORLD DO YOU THINK YOUR ARE?

Look at the political climate of the world. Everyone is into peace and unity and caring and all that. You've got the right party line—you just need the right party to get your message on-line. You need exposure, baby, big-time exposure, and I think I might be the guy to do it. That "turn the other cheek bit" works great in the antigun, nonviolent, pacifistic, love-the-planet, pantywaist phase we're in now. You could get some good mileage out of turning cheeks.

But Christ, lighten up on the biggies, like adultery, fornication, five-nication (Jesus, I'm only kiddin'), same-sex marriages, abortion. Avoid the hot buttons, baby, and we can get this messiah thing back off the ground. The world needs someone like you, but, quite honestly, you need me. I can make you a star, Jesus. Just hook your little wagon to me and my machine, and we're gonna go places.

THERE IS A WAY THAT SEEMS RIGHT TO MEN....

This all sounds like just the right plan. Bring back a fading superstar to a planet that could really use a lift. A little light, some hope. A great ballad or two.

BUT THE END IS DESTRUCTION.

As crass as that slimy little soliloquy sounds, it really isn't far from how we want to manage our own personal Jesus in our day-to-day affairs. We are fond of what He's all about, but we just don't think He manages things the way that will get us the most bang for our buck. A "10 percent of the gross" deal is no small chunk of change, so we really should do more to milk our Jesus property for all He's worth.

MANAGING
OUR OWN PERSONAL JESUS

We need to carefully manage Him to make Him meet our needs as we carefully let Him meet the rest of our world. There must be a clever way to repackage this golden oldie. Like the manager said: He's really on to the right things; He just picked too many of the wrong things to make it big these days. Simplify, but stay global. A universal Jesus with many paths to the truth. Many truths.

NO TRUTH

But Jesus was not about big business, show business, or even His own business. He was all about His Father's business—nothing more, nothing less.

With the authority and credentials He carried, He could've worked some pretty spectacular things on the side to get a little more in His pockets before He went and died. But that was not and is not Jesus' style. He was God, and He was man. He came to earth with a simple plan. It wasn't even His. It was His Dad's. I'm sure He had some amazing ideas of His own, but He chose to log on to the will of the one who had more authority than He did. He honored the will of the one who sent Him more than He honored His own dreams and needs. Jesus freely and frankly told the players of His day His own restrictions:

THE SON CAN DO NOTHING BY HIMSELF;

HE CAN DO ONLY WHAT HE SEES HIS FATHER DOING,

BECAUSE WHATEVER THE FATHER DOES THE SON ALSO DOES.

www.john @5.19.com/niv

He said the same thing many different ways, many different times. And if Jesus, the Son of God, was willing to die to His dreams by logging on to the will of the creator of dreams, then that is something we may want to take very seriously. Jesus came to this world not only to pay the price for our imperfections in the giving of His life, but also to model the behavior and lifestyle He wanted us to live. Exquisitely and humbly—in life and in death. And death under God's arrangements seem to come early and often.

NOBODY SAID IT WOULD BE EASY. BUT IT TRULY IS FREEING. WHEN YOU B E L I E V E.

All you have read up to this point points to a simple progression. Believe. Listen. Obey. Die. Live again. Return to main menu. This is no easy task. But nobody really feels too good about easy anyway. The things of real value take the most work and sacrifice.

PEOPLE ARE DYING TO BELIEVE. JESUS DID.

Jesus had a lot to say about dying and giving, losing and living. He said words that sounded great, but He also lived those words, and that makes *Him* great. He asked nothing of us that He did not do Himself. He lived a simple life of sacrifice so all the captives could be free—all who would believe.

A FREEDOM FIGHTER THROUGH AND THROUGH.

And He did believe. He believed that His Father truly loved Him and had the best in store for Him. He believed that by doing the will of His Father, He would find a rare fullness of life that can never be found by packing more things into more homes and more cars. Things seem to just add more hassles and more cares. In the end, who really cares? It's really more about who we are than what we have. To live in the fullness of our being, we must first discover what it is to lose who we are and gain what is Him. For in Him, we live and breathe and have our being. In sin, we have death, decay and eyes unseeing.

YOKES ON YOU.

Jesus was and is the master of paradox. In terms of the world's logic, He was a clown with an uncanny way of turning the system upside down. He said, "Come unto me and I will give you rest" and "Take my yoke upon you, for my burden is light" What could be freeing about that? And what's a yoke?

THE JESUS
I NEVER
K   N   E   W.

He also said that whoever loses his life for Christ's sake will find it. Yeah, right. He commanded that we give and said that in our giving more would be given—back to us. Love your enemy, he said, and do good to those that hurt you or hate you. (Help me with that one.) Worst of all, He said "follow me"—but I can't see Him. He even told us that whatever we do, do it joyfully unto God. And that is what He did. He loved the poor. He gave them life, sight, health, forgiveness, and wealth. (No wait, that wealth thing was someone else.) He gave of His love and His time, and He moved freely through all social classes. He was a respecter of no one and a lover of all. Even kids. Especially kids—though kids are so insignificant, curious, and small.

He's a ruler of angels but a servant of men. He loved every sinner—and made hookers his friends. He moved through the people; He healed lepers and bleeders. He loves cross-dressers, cross-bearers, homos, and breeders. Remember, if He can love me, He can love you.

Detained on His way to see a friend sick in bed, He cried for a while, then brought life to the dead. He found tax guys and fishermen to teach what He taught, while leaving the right and religious cold and distraught. He gave salvation, forgiveness, and freedom for free. To all who received, for all who believed.

Who was this Jesus who turned lives upside down?

A MADMAN, A PROPHET, A GOD, OR A CLOWN?

Jesus was a perfect Son to a perfect Father. He loved His dad with all His heart. "I and my Father are one," He said. But to live a life of obedience through glory and shame, this Jesus had to trust beyond belief to see life past the grave.

DEAD MAN WALKING.

And He did, you know. He loved His Father so much that He obeyed. He trusted His Father so much that He entered the grave with no guarantees other than what He believed. And He believed. Now He is asking us to do the same. This same Jesus is asking us to follow His lead. To risk it all, including all that we love, all that we value, and all we believe. And if we do, we will truly see.

ONE THING I KNOW: I WAS BLIND, BUT NOW I SEE.

What we will see is often more difficult to believe than what we couldn't see when we first chose to believe. We will see shattered lives put back together—not shattered dreams glued all cobweblike back into some tragic frame, but new dreams in their place that speak more clearly to the core of who we are and who we are going to be. In

Him. He raises the dead even today. And if we allow Him the opportunity, when we log on to His page—to His will—we will become like dead men walking. Dead men, waking.

On the Pop CD, Bono, of U2 fame, sings a haunting tune that calls for resurrection. To my understanding, it's a ballad that begs us to become like Jesus and walk into the resurrection round that will bring real life to the masses. To slow and mysterious music, Bono's haunting voice cries out to Jesus for help. He asks to hear the story about eternity and how it's all going to come out. He sings of the emptiness and loneliness and the messed up state our world is in—that we are in—so wake up, dead man, and help. Maybe he is crying out to us for help. Maybe its time these dead men woke and in the waking will come to help. Wake up, dead man. W A K E.

When we wake to our new life in Him, we discover that the gifts and talents that have been woven into our fabric are set in motion in strange new ways—ways that will stir others' emotions and give them a notion of what it is like to be free. And to see other captives come clean.

But first comes death and a willingness to continue to die. Then, just as you asked Him to speak, ask Him to speak purpose and destiny into your dreams. Allow Him to give you a vision of who you will be and what that will mean to a world so in need.

Before our personal resurrection, you and I were nothing more than zombies, looking to things and people and places on which to feed. We weren't designed to be parasitic beings sucking all the life from the things around us. We were called to be life givers, freedom fighters, kingdom builders, and truth tellers.

> I HAVE RAISED HIM UP IN RIGHTEOUSNESS,
> AND I WILL DIRECT ALL HIS WAYS; HE SHALL
> BUILD MY CITY AND LET MY EXILES GO FREE...
>
> www.isaiah@45.13.com/nkjv

WAKE UP, DEAD MAN

As you move into your own resurrection, you will see with resurrected eyes. You will touch lives with resurrected hands—hands filled with healing, power, sweat, and grace. You will feel what Jesus feels, and your blood, your shared blood with your Father, will pump through your resurrected veins and heart. And from your heart, your mouth will speak. You will speak with tongues of men and angels, and your new ears will hear the voice of God. As a result, you will see other dead men waking and walking—and together we will set the captives free.

But first you must become a son, a child of the perfect Father who wants you to become all that He intended you to be. Unique. Ironically, the religious system of Jesus' day put Him to death because

He called Himself a son—the Son of God. **Blasphemy!** It was that act of stepping into the role of a son that cost Him His life. It will cost you yours, too, but resurrection is on the other side. And that's real life and real living. As a dead man waking, you'll give a blind and barren world a chance to see Jesus in many different shapes and forms—resurrected forms taking shape in you and me. In so doing, we will walk boldly into our inheritance and invite those we meet to walk boldly into theirs.

The world takes notice when there is a dead man walking. For more than two thousand years, people have been talking about just such a man. But, if you haven't noticed, it has grown rather quiet as of late. Let's give them something to talk about.

WAKE UP,
DEAD MAN
WAKE

AFTERWORDS 6.0
SAFE SIX

LOVE AND COMPASSION CAN TAKE YOU
BEHIND ENEMY LINES AND WIN EVEN THE MOST
FORTIFIED CITIES.

THE TROJAN FORCE

Love never fails. Lust forever fuels…more lust. Even with resurrected bodies, hearts, and minds, we may find that some parts of our bodies are quick to step out of line. Old habits die hard, and dying to ourselves is not a once-and-for-all proposition. It's something we have to do over and over again. I die a thousand deaths when it comes to sex.

As I write this chapter, I find myself again in the killing fields after stepping stupidly in a fresh patch of old-fashioned lust. The good news is that nothing was planted; nothing was sown; no fruit was eaten; and nothing lurid has grown. I just got my feet a little dirty as I ran naked through the passion playgrounds of my mind.

We live in an excessively erotic culture, where love has been pawned cheaply for lust. Falling in love translates loosely into "falling in lust." Falling in love is like falling upstairs. It is possible—I've seen people do it, and they look really stupid. You have to work your way into love. It isn't a feeling or a phase. It's a decision based on an amalgamation of emotions, logic, companionship, trust, devotion, and, finally, passion. Love is a place of vulnerability where you put yourself on the line for another to inspect and either embrace or reject. We all fear rejection. But we fear being alone even more, so we step timidly out there where bullets fly and loves are lost. For this rare gift, we'll pay the cost.

Despite these precautionary words, this is not a chapter on the perils of promiscuity or the seduction of sex. I just used this opportunity to bump up the ratings by appealing to your prurient interests to get you to read on and read about the virtues of the most important virtue of all.

We continually confuse love with lust and love with sex. I thought it might help you to know that you are not alone in this confusing hormonal war zone. Every form of media leads us to believe that we can be happy and fulfilled only when we are lost in the embrace of another human being. (Preferably a supermodel with a high IQ and money to burn.) But what everyone in the world really longs for is unconditional love—love that is given freely and lavishly with no strings attached. A love like this is hard to find—a love so pure it lasts through time. There is one who can give it—the one who gave it and lived it and continually gives it.

WE ALL SEEM WILLING TO DIE FOR LOVE, BUT JESUS ACTUALLY DID.

Even more than dying for love, He lived for love. He made

love the cornerstone of everything He claimed, everything He
preached, everything He believed. Love became the greatest commandment of all. It is what He requires of you and me: to love while learning to allow ourselves to be loved—to know, even as we are known.

A NEW COMMANDMENT I GIVE TO YOU, THAT YOU LOVE ONE
ANOTHER, AS I HAVE LOVED YOU…BY THIS ALL WILL KNOW THAT
YOU ARE MY DISCIPLES, IF YOU HAVE LOVE FOR ONE ANOTHER.

www.john@13.34–35.com/nkjv

Jesus went on to say that if you truly love God, you will
obey His commands. This is not about laws; it's about love and trust. It
means you are willing to believe that the one who made you knows
more about what is good for you than you do. And that is hard to
believe.

IF ANYONE LOVES ME, HE WILL KEEP MY WORD; AND MY
FATHER WILL LOVE HIM, AND WE WILL COME TO HIM AND MAKE
OUR HOME WITH HIM. HE WHO DOES NOT LOVE ME DOES NOT
KEEP MY WORDS; AND THE WORD WHICH YOU HEAR IS NOT
MINE BUT THE FATHER'S WHO SENT ME.

www.john@14.23–24.com/nkjv

Once again Jesus shows that the power and authority that come
from these words are the result of His being a son. Now He commands
that we love. In this comes freedom, not bondage. Real life, not death.

LoVe is the PiTs.

I love my pit bull, Erich. He is ninety-five pounds of love and five pounds of stink. All he wants is to love, be loved, and to please me. But true to his breed, he is bullheaded, obstinate, and selectively deaf. My friends claim he takes after me.

Erich and I live in a loft on the rooftop of the old Pabst Brewery in downtown Los Angeles. Although we have thousands of square feet of deck space, a little garden, and views that make your heart race, Erich acquired the bad habit of frequenting the backside of the studio, where there is a foul, cavernous underbelly filled with billions of filthy pigeons.

Erich took a liking to those dirty birds (although I don't think they liked him back). He found every imaginable way to get to them. When I came home from work, I smelled the pungent odor of pigeons all over him. In the middle of the night, I felt fleas all over us. (It is an ugly thing to be this honest—to confess that I sleep with a pit bull. But there is a point—I promise.)

I spent day after day building walls and barriers to keep Erich free of disease. He spent an equal amount of time undoing what I had done. When I saw feathers sticking out of his lips and his ears, my outbursts of rage shocked even me. I spanked him maybe a few thousand times, if you have to know the truth. But nothing could dissuade

Erich from his mission. Again and again, he returned to the pigeon pit like an addict in search of a fix.

I realized that Erich had no idea why I wanted to prevent him from hanging out with his new "homings." He could never have understood that I was only protecting him from stench, disease, and all those stupid fleas. I love that big, stinky dog. I want him to have friends; I want him to have fun; but I also want him around for as long as possible. I finally constructed a barrier so Erich-tight that he couldn't possibly hang with his foul feathered friends.

And whether he gets it or not, I will continue to lay down the law, so I can live flea-free with a healthy dog.

One day, it dawned on me: Erich and I are not so different. Though the objects of my affection are not pigeons, there are plenty of things I'm drawn to that seem insanely fun, but which lead to destruction. I don't have to list the lifestyles that lead to addiction, death, and disease. They are all around us. Like stupid fleas.

When I finally understood that I could never really understand, it made me appreciate and respect God's tough commands—even though I have trouble abiding by some of them. He cares enough to keep us healthy and disease free. He loves us enough to protect us from our own destructive desires, despite how much we fight Him on those fronts. It's frustrating to be loved so much. I think Erich might agree.

GODDOG

SOMETIMES WE JUST NEED A MIRROR TO HELP US SEE.

As we begin to move in obedience born of love, we see God make His home in us. And as He begins to live in us, His love flows naturally through us. Love covers a multitude of sins, and love—when used properly—turns enemies into friends

IN LOVE AND WAR

An insane war rages in our world. It is waged to keep God's creation in bondage, oppression, and fear. The pain it produces has left many people scarred and scared and cowering behind walls of guilt and shame. Some of these walls are virtually impenetrable. Many of them don't look like walls at all, which makes them difficult to distinguish, much less destroy.

But there is a force—a **Trojan force**—that will break through even the most fortified of fears. If we live inside this Trojan force of love, we will find ourselves fast inside the lives and hearts of the ones we fought and feared. When we give others genuine love—with no hidden agendas or ulterior motives (like a multilevel marketing scheme to line your pockets or fill your pews)—we dissolve the barriers to their hearts. And when we do, we often find that the only fight that's left is a fight to hold back tears as we embrace our former-foes-turned-newfound-friends.

Sounds too good to be true. It is, and it's true.

LOVE RECKLESSLY.

For the past five or six years I have traveled the world interviewing young people from all over the planet. I learned a little secret that has allowed me behind the iron walls of white supremacist hideouts in New Zealand, into the hearts of gang kids in East L. A., and into the throne rooms of some minikings of our day. The "secret" is called love, and it is and always has been the greatest power in the world.

Love is the premise of everything that God embodies. Love led to Creation and cost God His only Son. This mystifying love breaks down the walls of separation—the walls we build to keep, "them" out and "us" in. Jesus called us to go out and love, but our walls keep most of us out of action in a world dying to be loved. If we could only tap into that love—real, sacrificial, supernatural love—we could move behind every wall imaginable to touch even the most unreachable with a love that is unfathomable. How in the world is that possible?

ASK FOR IT BY NAME.

Early one morning in 1994, I asked God for something that nearly destroyed me. I have a reputation for loving strangers. Frankly, I'm a goon magnet. If there is a wacky person within a five-mile radius, he will somehow find me. I guess this is because I really do love people, and everyone wants to be loved. But it's usually only the goons who are willing to let you know. I should know; I'm one of them.

My friend John used to come to my apartment every morning, and we would hang out and talk with God. On this particular morning, just before I left for Eastern Europe to travel with a punk band, I asked God to allow me to feel what He feels for people—to feel what He feels for those who are hurting, lonely, and desperate.

It was an innocent prayer uttered in sincerity, but it turned out to be more than I had bargained for. Instantly, God granted my request. Tears poured down my face, and I couldn't make them stop. My buddy John looked a little alarmed.

It was as if God allowed me to feel an ounce of the pain He feels for His creation—in every land and every nation. If you multiply that twinge of pain by the number of His sons and daughters, you can imagine that it would feel very much like a slaughter.

Much to John's relief, I eventually pulled myself together. I had learned a powerful lesson. What I realized was that God feels immeasurably more than we could ever be capable of feeling. What He feels is love, and with love often comes pain. Real pain. Deep pain.

A few days after that odd encounter with the God of the universe, I found myself on the border of Poland and Russia in an old World War II military installation. At that bizarre venue a band called "No Longer Music" put on a punk opera to introduce kids to God.

After a late performance, I stood face-to-face with a kid who was very high on something very strong. He screamed obscenities and spit in my face. Under normal circumstances, it would have been easy not to love him. But, as you've undoubtedly gathered, these were not normal circumstances.

Suddenly, my early morning prayer kicked in. I had been trying to argue a point with this kid about the existence of God and the logic of an illogical world. Then, in an instant, there were no more words. Despite the vulgarities and abuse he hurled at me, I felt nothing but love for him. Intense, painful love.

Tears filled my eyes as I told him, "You know, you have a good heart."

He stopped, and for a moment his eyes cleared. "I know," he said in strained English.

"And I love you," I continued, feeling God's broken heart.

He stared at me to make sure *I* wasn't high. Then tears filled his eyes. From that point on, the message was clear and few words were spoken. Words, arguments, theories, and doctrines were no match for the love that bathed this man—a love served fresh from the God he despised and delivered by some random guy. Who can defend against the Trojan force of love?

The scene gets hazy for me after that. It was late; I was tired; and the profound emotion made me feel wasted and spent. But I know

one thing for certain—a battle was won and a life was changed that
night in an old war camp. I don't know for sure what happened to the
Polish kid.

Ever since I asked God to allow me to feel what He feels for
His children, I have frequently come off looking like a total kook. Like
the time I gave a flight attendant a copy of *The Message* simply
because I felt God telling me to—only to see her kneeling and crying at
my seat an hour later.

"Why did you give this to me?" she asked. "I was staring in
the mirror before this flight, and I decided I was going to end it all.
Now this."

While riding a bus from New Jersey to Manhattan, I sat behind
the driver, a huge African-American man with salt-and-pepper hair. After
talking for a while, I told him how great it is to be in a relationship with
the God of the universe. Just before we pulled into the city, he asked the
other passengers if he and I could get off the bus for a minute. There out
on the street, looking over the George Washington Bridge, this driver
asked God to be his friend and Father. (I figured if the other riders were
late for appointments, that was just too bad. What could be more important than a lifesaving appointment with the **Creator?**)

One afternoon recently, while on a crash-and-burn deadline
for a video project, my thoughts were interrupted by a divine directive to
call a television producer in New York and tell him that Jesus loves

him—no matter what he was into or what he had done. I felt like a fool, since this is something I would rarely tell even a friend. When I finally followed through, I heard this man, a man I hardly knew, get choked up on the other end of the phone, on the other side of the country.

"Why did you call at this moment to tell me that?" he asked. "You have no idea what I'm going through and the ways I've messed up."

He was right—I had no idea. In fact, I didn't know if he was a Hindu, Baptist, Buddhist, or Jew. Apparently it doesn't matter. Jesus isn't into brands. He simply loves us all, and just then, especially, He loved that man.

As exciting as these accounts may sound, I could tell you story after story of how pathetic and foolish I have looked while looking through new eyes, with His heart, at one of God's broken kids. If you want to attempt this, it is only fair to warn you: You will make a lot of mistakes when you move in this dimension. But the risks are less risky when it's His love that you mention.

Still, as ridiculous as I have sometimes appeared, the rewards have far exceeded the costs. It is risky to feel so deeply for those you do not know. But you will never understand how much God cares until you let Him flow from His heart through your heart to theirs. You will see hearts melt and lives change before your very eyes. And whether you like it or not, you'll learn how often our God cries.

He does, you know.

PLEASURE AND PAIN

THE DARK SIDE OF LOVE.

Here's something you may never have considered: We are very frail beings to harbor God-sized love. This powerful force will flow through you without notice and when you least expect it. It is impossible to contain it, and if you're not careful you may misread it. If you don't, the recipient may. There are always complications to these things. Let's face it, most of us mishandle strong emotions and deep feelings. We muddle our motives and goof up our good intentions.

As I mentioned earlier, love and lust are so closely connected in our minds and twisted by the media that sometimes this overpowering feeling can make us think it is something other than pure love with no strings attached for whomever it is you may happen to be with. We all have certain human needs, and we can pervert or tarnish something that is genuine and meant to be free. If we don't check ourselves, a flawless kind of God-love can slide into lust.

BURNING DOWN THE HOUSE.

I'm writing this chapter at a friend's cabin in the California mountains in a tiny village called Twin Peaks. Last night was a near **fire walk** with me. I had been working on this chapter about love, so I decided to sit by the fire and spend time sharing some love with my dog. After an hour, I turned off the fire (it was gas) and went to bed. About twenty minutes later, just as I was hovering between the waking world and dreams, I heard the soothing sound of crackling embers. There was that sweet smell of smoke in the mountain air. It was so nice. AND SO WRONG!

Yanked from my semiconscious state, I thought, *Wait a minute; gas logs don't crackle, and they don't smoke. Besides, I turned the fire off.*

I leaped out of bed, sprinted to the living room, and found that the inside wall above the firebox had caught on fire. In a few McMinutes this beautiful cabin, my friend's beautiful cabin, was going to be a pile of ashes. I ran around looking for hoses, extinguishers, anything that would spray. I used them all, but the fire continued to blaze.

AN A.D.D. MOMENT

do not spray Windex through tiny cracks in cabin walls in an attempt to put out large blazes. it is a huge waste of time and Windex

Thank You

There was no phone, so I had to run half-dressed to the nearest cabin to make a call. I must have looked like a deranged character from a Stephen King movie when I pounded on the neighbor's door.

The overspray of Windex on my torso made the white powder from the fire extinguisher stick to my body, giving me the look of a mad mime with bleached white hair. (At least I wasn't carrying an ax.)

Fortunately, people living in the mountains are amazingly friendly to near naked strangers at weird kinds of hours.

A few weeks later, the fire department came and stopped the blaze. They had to remove an exterior wall to thoroughly douse the fire. I wanted them to leave it intact so the damage wouldn't look so bad. Maybe my friend wouldn't be so alarmed—maybe he wouldn't even know that his cabin had nearly burned to the ground. But the fire-fighters had to make sure the blaze was out, so they did their demolition job. Predictably, it looked like a mess, and my friend was shocked, but the cabin—sans charred wall—still stands.

I tell you all of this because it made me take seriously the battle we all face with lust. Earlier in this chapter I spoke loosely about my own careless bouts with it. No damage done. But this morning as I woke from what I thought was a dream in a place that smelled of smoke, God, in a very vivid way, gave me a deeper understanding of the danger. There is a proverb that says something like this: If you take fire into your lap, you're going to get burned. I think that means that if you allow a little lust in, it will end up burning down your house. Passion is powerful. And we, for the most part, are not.

The fire chief said that the cabin fire was inevitable. The

firebox had been deteriorating, and even though no flames were in con-
tact with any wood, something called *pyrolysis* had taken effect.
Ongoing exposure to heat had lowered the combustion temperature of
the wood. Eventually, even the slightest heat would have caused that
wood to combust.

So it is with lust.

We are exposed over and over to images, music, and thoughts
that fan the flames of our passion. At some point, pyrolysis takes effect
in our inner structure, and our combustion temperature drops. Is it any
wonder that we find ourselves fighting the fiercest flames though it
seemed that the lust we were stirring was only an ember?

When you allow even a bit of inner deterioration in your life, it
takes just a tiny increase in heat for the whole thing to go up in flames.
Passion unchecked, or played off carelessly, can be more dangerous than
you ever thought. Once the fire starts, you will have to tear off your
facade to put out the flames completely and rebuild the insides. Everyone
will notice the mess. It's ugly, but it's necessary.

When you play with the fires of lust, you will get burned, or
you will burn someone else. And for some time thereafter you and your
dog will smell like smoke. There will be a big mess to clean up, and
you will have to tell your friend about his cabin.

A PERSONAL FIRESTORM

Not long ago, I endured one of the most painful years of my

life when I loved someone who couldn't be mine. I didn't understand why, but like Erich and his pigeons, I didn't need to understand; I just needed to obey. I had to leave someone I truly loved as an act of sacrifice to honor God—although it may have looked like an act of careless disregard.

The love I left would never believe that I left for a higher calling. The pain of loving someone who couldn't believe my love was genuine seemed to hurt even more than my broken heart—and I have never known a pain as intense as that of a broken heart.

On the one-year anniversary of the beginning of that unimaginable pain, while driving through the high desert of Nevada, I cried out to God, "Are you ever going to take this agony away?"

God gently spoke through my pain with this thought: *I may not. This is an important part of what you asked for when you asked to feel what I feel for those who don't know me. You are experiencing one instance of a love that cannot be—and the recipient of that love doesn't even believe that your love is true. I have countless millions of loves that will never be mine. And the ones denying my love do not even believe **I am real.** This, too, is an answer to your prayer. It is the painful side of love. And I've only given you a taste of what I feel.*

Just when you think you can take no more, His love comes in like a flood. His tears sometimes feel that way, too.

ALL THAT WATER ALLOWED

MY CABIN TO STAND. BUT

THE SMOKE STILL LINGERS AND

SOMETIMES I CAN STILL

SMELL THE SMOLDERING PAIN.

IT IS IMPORTANT TO REALIZE

HOW POWERFUL THIS

TROJAN FORCE CAN BE.

IF WE USE IT PURELY AND

PROPERLY, WE WILL SEE

CAPTIVES SET FREE.

AfterWords 7.0
POWER 2 THE PEOPLE
IN A POWER HUNGRY WORLD.

THE MASSES GET NASTY
WHEN THE POWER GOES OUT.

I know I do. And did. My stay in the mountains was cut short when the cabin fire melted the wiring, leaving me with little light. The food in the fridge was quickly moving west of fresh. I knew I would need to quickly move west as well because none of my writing felt fresh. Maybe it was the smell of smoke and the fire extinguisher powder that made it hard to clear my head. So after driving home to L.A., I boarded a plane for Chicago.

Ironically, the day I arrived in the Windy City, the newspaper headlines read: **Power Outage Keeps Chicago in the Dark.** How odd that, just when I was thinking and writing about power, I found myself in a city that had gone dark four times in a week. Suddenly, this power chapter began to flow through me as I watched the ramifications of a large-scale power loss play out before me.

According to the newspaper account, the unexplained power outages prompted easily explainable power oust-ages. The most recent blackout had cost Chicago businesses about one hundred million dollars, and the mayor made sure it cost the senior vice president of the power company his job. When those in power want to remain in power, they make sure they have the power in control. If not, you can be sure that heads will roll. In a city where you don't mess with the political machine, things and people fall in line. And today, Chicago was back on-line. And so am I. At least for another few days.

We all rely on power. We take it for granted, and we are dismayed when it isn't there. If my gadgets don't work when I plug them in, I feel paralyzed and panic-stricken. How we can be so dependent on something we cannot see, control, or create on our own?

Most of us don't really understand electricity, but that doesn't matter. We choose to believe that it will be there to make our air more breathable, our food less perishable, the temperature more tolerable, and our lives more livable. If you don't think power outages rile people up, spend time in a city that just lived through several in a short span of time. Tempers flair when temperatures soar, and so does the incidence of crime. When an urban center stays dark for days on end, mayhem ensues in Mad Max proportions.

KIND OF LIKE TODAY.

Many desperate people, including you and me, have been groping around in the dark. We've been lost, confused, and desperately seeking something to believe in and someone to light the way. Our world has never been darker, and a global power outage is to blame.

Jesus Unplugged.

REM's Michael Stipe sings an anthem celebrating the loss of his religion. He sings of paradox—of being first in the spotlight, then in the corner. In one moment he's said too much; in the next, he hasn't said enough. But the point is clear: He's losing his religion. And he seems to recommend that we do too.

I couldn't agree with him more. The truth is: Whether we've said too much or haven't said enough, we certainly haven't seen enough or felt enough, but we've definitely **heard** enough.

Enough.

We've heard plenty of talk from plastic people about a placid Jesus that leaves us profoundly peaceful about our profession of disinterest in a feeble, fruitless faith. An unplugged Jesus can't do much in a plugged-in, turned-on, fast-paced world.

Too many religious institutions have been proclaiming a powerless Jesus for far too long. No wonder this swiftly tilting planet is largely losing its religion as it embraces anything and everything else that projects power. An unplugged Jesus is not only boring and lifeless, He is just generally not worth worshiping or worrying about when so many other things on Planet Distraction are plugged in and playing at full bore, full time, and more. A powerless Jesus leaves me cold when Prodigy is pounding, and my heart is keeping the beat. Who can dance to the dirge of a two-thousand-year-old icon who can't in an age where everyone and everything else can—except this mild and powerless, bleeding old man?

GREAT IS OUR LORD, AND MIGHTY IN POWER.

www.psalm@147.5.com/niv

But can it be that this powerless figure has been poorly portrayed by those in the seats of religious power? Those in power wish to remain in power, and if real power threatens their control, then maybe the power itself has to go.

Since real power cannot be contained, controlled, or created, it is a frightening thing to purvey to a people in need. What if it is too much, not enough, not on time, or out of line? Power is a dangerous force. It cannot be forced or coerced.

True power from on high is power that will electrify, and when it is present, you cannot stand by unaffected. It's electric; it's divine; and it is always right on time. Never early, never late. Our God sometimes wants to make us wait. It is all about Him and not about us. It's all about His power and our willingness to trust.

I don't know about you, but I'm happy to lose my religion if it means saying good-bye to empty rituals and fading icons that say, "I can't." I don't want leaders, teachers, preachers, or anyone else selling me a version of God that is anything less than He really is.

What if the **real** Jesus, the God we never knew, was always there and always true? What if we've been kept in the dark while we listened to the right, and the left, and the religious bark? Like the carnies that roll into town to get what they can while they shake us all down. They use colorful lights on fast-spinning rides; they sell us tickets and junk food and sugar spun wide. We shouldn't be shocked, amazed, or surprised. When the power outage hits, the looters will thrive.

Chaos rules when darkness falls. And God won't fit in man-made walls. The games we've played in Jesus' name are rigged and bogus, and the prize is lame. An unplugged Jesus, plastic and small, that looks like junk on anyone's wall. I want my money back. Keep your religious bric-a-brac. We're all sick of this obvious, powerless con.

PLEASE, FOR THE SAKE OF US ALL, TURN THE POWER BACK ON.

MEN SHALL SPEAK OF THE MIGHT OF YOUR AWESOME ACTS, AND I WILL DECLARE YOUR GREATNESS.

www.psalm@145.6.com/nkjv

Throughout time, religious systems have failed because of those operative words: religious and systems. We have listened to church growth plans that involve clever schemes to bring in the lost. Often those schemes just bring in the lust—lust for more members, lust for bigger and better buildings, and lust for the power that comes when the numbers increase. But Jesus, the flesh and blood Jesus, cared nothing for those things.

Instead, He moved in a love that had real power to change lives. The power was the thing that brought the people in droves to experience miracles. But the sheer power of His message also drove many away.

We live in a world that has seen it all but experienced little of the power that resides in the presence of the King. Power that we *all* have access to as sons and daughters of the Most High God. Power that is there for the taking for those who will receive it. And power that will change the hearts and minds of those who won't. But first they must see.

BUT FIRST, WE MUST BELIEVE.

Pawn your plastic Jesus. Put away your fears and your preconceived notions of who God is and what He can do through you. There is power beyond your wildest dreams when you allow the God of the universe to become Lord of those dreams. Speaking of dreams:

AND AFTERWARD, I WILL POUR OUT MY SPIRIT ON

ALL PEOPLE. YOUR SONS AND YOUR

DAUGHTERS WILL PROPHESY,

YOUR OLD MEN WILL DREAM DREAMS,

YOUR YOUNG MEN WILL SEE VISIONS...

I WILL POUR OUT MY SPIRIT IN THOSE DAYS.

I WILL SHOW WONDERS IN THE HEAVENS

AND ON THE EARTH...

www.joel@.2.28–30.com/niv

Dreams and visions are an important part of being interactive with God. He often chooses to speak to us boldly in vivid pictures, visions, and digital dreams—so much better than HDTV or DVD on big plasma screens.

I guess the password is and will always be:

B E L I E V E.

Not too long ago, I began to believe—really believe—in the power of God. But even before I did, He allowed me to catch a glimpse of just how amazingly He can act through us. I hadn't even asked to be a conduit for His power. But I think He wanted me to, so He did that little DJ thing where you begin to hear a sample of the next song mixed into the song you are dancing to, so you get an idea of what is coming next. I heard part of a powerful song late one night while writing a paper for a graduate school class.

My deadline was coming with the light of the next day, and my thoughts seemed to be moving more slowly than the sun. But God was more concerned with a son going down than the sun coming up. Even as my deadline approached, God spoke a thought I couldn't ignore:

"Go ask your neighbor, Stephen, if he is considering suicide."

This was before I realized that God still speaks directly to people. So I decided this was a clever diversion of my own making to keep me from the job at hand. Even though my A.D.D. is chronic, I knew this was not a common distraction.

"No, this is nuts," was my terse reply. "I don't even know that guy." But God did. And He wanted His power to flow and His love to shine.

A NEAR FATAL DISTRACTION

God was relentless, and the battle raged for hours. He told me to go, and I said no. This was a war of the wills. He had the advantage. He could mess with my head, which made it tough for me to write. Still, I wouldn't budge. After all, my neighbor and I had met just the week before, and it was only in passing.

But God wasn't passing.

"God, this just can't be a good way to win friends and influence people," I continued to protest. "Besides, what am I supposed to say? 'Hi, remember me? We met last week. You're not thinking about killing yourself, are you?'"

That approach sounded more like a suggestion than an indication of concern. I couldn't do it. It was pride suicide. I had to spare my reputation and my grades. I was pretty sure my professor would never believe I couldn't finish my paper because I was on a mission from God.

At two in the morning, I walked outside to get some air and try to clear my mind and conscience for ignoring that strong prompt to talk to a guy I barely knew about something I could not know.

Then something caught my eye. There in the empty street I spotted Stephen's dog. If I didn't return the dog, he might be lost or dead by morning. This dog gone scenario pushed me to the door I had avoided all night.

BEWARE OF DOG

With dog in tow, I knocked on my neighbor's door. I could hear pounding music, and voices carried into the dingy hall. Stephen's flatmates were throwing a party, so they received my awkward appearance at that late hour far better than I could've hoped.

One of the party people led me inside. "Hey, thanks for saving Elvis," he said. "Grab a drink—there's a bunch of stuff in the cooler."

I saw Stephen across the room, and after a few minutes he motioned for me to join him on the fire escape, where he lit up a smoke. The wind moved the power lines dangerously close to our rusted metal perch. I don't know which scared me more, the threat of man-made power, or God's. We leaned against the cold brick, silent for a long time. Stephen's cigarette glowed as he took a long drag. As he exhaled, he began his sad story and ushered me into his world of alcoholism and lost love.

At what I felt to be the most opportune time in an outlandish assignment, I looked him straight in the eye and asked, "Are you considering suicide?"

Dead silence.

Stephen took one long, last drag before the moment of truth. My heart raced and my throat went dry as he glared at me. He flicked the glowing cigarette off the building as he moved toward me. He began to shake.

"Who put you up to this?" he asked with a sneer.

He grabbed my shirt and pushed me up against the wall. This time with desperation and sincere angst in his voice, he shouted, *"Who told you to say that?"*

I began to shake. My part had been fairly easy up till now, but there was only one line in my script. *Okay, God, what do I say next?*

All I could do was tell the truth.

"I know it sounds crazy," I said, "but God told me."

He looked incredulous at first, making me almost want to back down and tell him this had been a big mistake. But there was nowhere more credible to go.

"Stephen, God must love you very much if He would prompt a perfect stranger to interrupt the writing of an imperfect paper to crash a party to let you know He cares," I said, sounding even crazier.

I saw a tear glisten in the match light as Stephen lit another smoke. For the next few hours, he talked about his dark depression and his dangerous dance with suicide over the past two weeks. We climbed down the fire escape and walked out into the empty street. Nothing was said for a very long time.

Finally, I told him again about his Father who loved Him and cared enough to send someone to tell him so.

Stephen threw his arms around me and would not let go. I'm big on hugging, but even I felt uncomfortable after the fourteenth minute of that hug, especially when a police car rolled slowly by. Certainly, that was no regular hug. It was a life-and-death embrace, and this guy was not about to let go. I think it was then that *I* began to learn to let go.

That night I learned I would much rather witness the death of my pride than contribute to a massive power outage that results in the death of an amazing child of God. God's power was flowing, and I had tried my hardest to make Him channel it in some other direction.

Eventually, Stephen loosened his grip on me and ran back toward his building. But he stopped in the middle of the street that was glowing with the promise of another tomorrow.

"God sent you!" he yelled to me with a hint of laughter in his voice. "He did, you know. God sent you to tell me. Thanks."

I have never felt so good, even though I knew my paper would not be finished on time. But so what? God had taught me far more than any term paper or class ever could. I had received an up close look at His plan. And although I may be a slow learner—a member of God's Special Ed.—I'm discovering that His plan is all that matters.

People are outraged during massive power outages. And that is why there has been so much anger misdirected at God. Desperation, despair, and self-destructive acts are the signs that a powerless planet has missed out on God's incredible plan. But don't be fooled—God will not be unplugged. Chances are, He will do the unplugging, and His outages can be felt around the globe. Maybe that explains the dwindling numbers who darken the doors of dark and powerless places where people wearily worship an impotent God.

IMMORAL SUPPORT

The moral of this story is that God cares enough to send a random power surge into a dark night to tap into our hearts and lives, whether we want Him to or not. His power is real and ready to be accessed. That night with Stephen, I heard the sample of a powerful song that has inspired me to dance dangerously close to insanity—at least as some perceive it.

I could tell you countless stories of flight attendants, television hosts, corporate heads, gang members, and restaurant servers whom God has asked me to serve—by loving, listening, and delivering mail from the God of the universe to His desperate children in need. We all need power, and we all need love. God is both, and that's enough.

If you think this is far-fetched or a supernatural stretch, just pick up the book that chronicles Jesus' life. Page after page tells of the miracles He performed. He healed the sick, brought the dead back to life, and made legions of demons flee.

And, most incredibly, He loved those whom no one else would or could. That is possible even for you and me. When we move in that dimension of love mixed with power, the captives will go free.

NOW MAY THE GOD OF HOPE FILL YOU

WITH ALL JOY AND PEACE IN BELIEVING,

THAT YOU MAY ABOUND IN HOPE

BY THE POWER OF THE HOLY SPIRIT.

www.paul@romans15.13.com/nkjv

Jesus lived on the edge and did incredible things. But He made a claim that is still hard to believe, especially in light of our dark and powerless world: "In my name you will do even greater works than these." The only question left to ask is:

WAS HE PLAYING WHEN HE SAID THAT, OR ARE WE???

AfTERWoRDs 8.0
ID oL WORSHIP
AND A HARD HARD RAIN
Is GonnaFall.

Before **rain** was even a vapor in the imagination of man, it was first a threat of judgment upon the land.

AND A HARD RAIN'S GONNA FALL.

There was a time, near the dawn of mankind, that the filth of violence and perversion filled the land. God allowed a power outage before His judgment fell swiftly and deftly on a dry and parched people in a sin-drenched land. I think you Noah what I'm talking about.

A HARD RAIN'S GONNA FALL.

Many years after God warned about the flood and issued redemptive instructions, man was introduced to rain in its thunderous fall of judgment. A hard rain did fall, and it took the whole of mankind with it, save Noah and his family. The heavy drops from heaven submerged the violence, the idolatry, and the perversion running rampant in that world. A torrential storm washed away all that was offensive— all that was a stench in the nostrils of a holy God.

I imagine that before the flood, Noah lost the respect of

those around him. They mocked and scorned the silly old man who insisted on building a giant ship when the only water for miles was deep in the wells of that arid place.

There was probably little support from anyone close to Noah in those days. After the first few decades, his family undoubtedly began to read up on Alzheimer's disease. And after fifty years of tedious labor on this undertaking, Noah may have questioned his sanity as much as his neighbors did.

But the rain did come.

And thank God for you and me, Noah endured. For through his tenacious belief, we were spared. Thank God that old man was willing to continue to build in the face of adversity. Thank God he listened. He made time to hear God, and he was foolish enough to believe.

Sometimes God's instructions are clear and direct, as through an audible voice, a burning bush, or an early morning wake-up call. Sometimes God's warnings are a little more nebulous, and He expects us to take note of the signs around us. He told us to pay attention to the seasons and the weather—even to the rain.

Despite God's promise to Noah and to all of mankind—a vow that he would never again use rain to flood the earth—on several occasions He has used a *lack* of it to make a point. Like words, rain can bring life, abundance, and healing. It can wash away the grime and bring a freshness and vitality that causes deserts to bloom and fields to bear fruit. Too much rain, and you have chaos in Titanic proportions. Not enough, and death is just as sure but not as swift.

Rain, like a word, has power.

There is also power in the latter rain—the reign of the Spirit that the Jesus People sang about in the late '60s and early '70s.

SEND THE RAIN, THE LATTER RAIN; SEND THE RAIN; RAIN ON ME THE LATTER RAIN—YOUR SPIRIT REIGN—LET IT FALL; LET IT WASH OVER ME.

I remember that when I was a boy, we used to hold meetings in the basement of the little duplex where my family lived. Ten to fifteen people sang and worshiped with no thought for tomorrow. That made sense to me because I was never sure there would be a tomorrow.

Films such as *Thief in the Night* and *A Distant Thunder* were in circulation in those days. I could never sleep after seeing those horrifying end-times films. In one, everyone disappeared inexplicably in a rapture of glory, and in the other they had their heads chopped off for sticking around and taking the mark of the beast: 666. To me, it was a lose-lose proposition.

HELLO? ANYBODY HOME?

As a result, I never let my parents get too far out of my sight. On rare occasions when I would come home from school to find the house empty, I always expected the worst. Instead of worrying about the basics, like what would I eat, I always wondered how long I could avoid the guillotine. Those films scared the hell out of me. I guess that was the point.

Despite our naivete in our "Jesus People daze," the rain fell in meeting after meeting. The music and worship lasted long into the night. Each gathering was a marathon session of joyful praise, where young and old basked in the latter rain of the Spirit. Warm drops of mercy set our hearts free.

It's been a while since I've seen that kind of rain. It's becoming a memory trace, sepia-toned and fading fast. Things seem pretty dry, and the hearts of man seem to mirror the cracked, parched soil in our sin-drenched land.

What has happened to the rain?

Mark Twain said that everyone talks about the weather, but nobody does anything about it. Well, maybe it's time we do something about the lack of precipitation in our land. Maybe it's time we stop talking—stop our idol chatter—and start doing.

I want to do something about the dryness that consumes this spiritually arid desert. I want to see the floodgates of heaven open and pour down heavy drops. Maybe it has nothing to do with the weather and everything to do with our idols—the idols that have captured our imagination, passion, and time.

Let's turn our attention to another dry spell, a time of kings and priests and the dancing prophets of Baal. A time when the people turned from their God to worship gods of their own making—gods with mouths that couldn't speak and ears that couldn't hear. Those gods may have looked appealing on the movie posters, billboards, and CD inserts, but they had no power.

NO REIGN
N O   R A I N
THE ELIJAH PROJECT

Elijah, the great Old Testament prophet, ran headlong into the same problem we have today. The people had grown bored with the one true God and were courting all the rest. But our God is a jealous lover. Jesus' commands make it clear that He doesn't want to share our affection with anyone or anything. Love the Lord your God with all your heart. Set no other gods before me. And love your neighbor as yourself. The rest are just the details.

DETACHABLE JESUS

It seems that we have not only neglected the details, but we have forgotten the main points as well. We have somehow found ourselves a detachable Jesus we can put on and take off at will. When He is inconvenient, we put Him away, but we take Him out to share with our friends from church. When He is politically incorrect, we slip Him into the drawer with our *What would Jesus wear?* and our tasty Test-a-Mints. Then we take Him out again when we are in the lurch.

This can't be what the King of Kings had in mind when He commanded us to take up our crosses and follow Him. And it surely couldn't be what Paul meant when he said, "I die daily."

It would be a little more like saying: You can have all this—and Jesus, too!

He wants us to love Him like we love a boyfriend, girlfriend, husband, or wife. How is it that we have chosen to love Him like we love our grandmother? It's as if we know He appreciates a call now and then, and our parents love Him, so we guess we should too. But how long do we actually have to talk? And what on earth do we have in common? Still, we keep calling and sending thank-you notes to make sure that the birthday and Christmas money keeps coming in. It's a good investment, really.

God isn't a grandma. He requires *our everything*—our complete devotion. He wants to know us intimately, and He yearns to spend quality and quantity time with us. He longs for time when we can listen and time when we can be. Together.

Unfortunately, today everything co-opts our time *but* Him. We are in love with our things, our friends, our careers, our cars. We want what's bigger and better, new and improved. We worship the same gods the rest of the world worships, and we know more about what stars are doing than what the *maker* of the stars is doing.

In the days of Elijah, the children of Israel and most of the adults were dancing with demons and living like them too. They had their eyes and hands on everything but the Eternal One and His plans. It was their rebellion, perversion, and idolatry that brought on the drought. Their sin permeated the nostrils of God and caused Him to restrain the rain. No rain, just famine and pain for a rebellious and hard-hearted people who had forgotten their God. Not a happy place to be. Not for them, not for Him, not for you, not for me.

WILL THE REAL GOD PLEASE STAND UP

Drastic times require drastic measures. Elijah knew it was time for a showdown. He called a meeting of the people—the Baal worshipers, their priests, and the children of Israel. The lines of distinction were terribly blurred, and the lines of the hungry got longer as the desiccation persisted for three bone-dry years.

Elijah proclaimed his challenge from high atop Mount Carmel: "How long will you waver between two opinions? If the Lord is God, follow Him; but if Baal is God, follow him." Like so many complacent audiences, before and since, the people yawned and said nothing. It was a tough crowd, and it was a pivotal time.

Even though the event was billed as a showdown of the gods, it was a real test of faith for Elijah. He knew that in the past His God had always come through. But confronting a hard-hearted crowd and nine hundred dancing pagan prophets is no time to be calling for spontaneous combustion—unless you know you'll be fired from on high.

NEVER YELL FIRE IN A CROWDED IDOL
LIFESTYLE UNLESS YOU
WANT TO GET BURNED.

But before Elijah called down the fire, he went back to the basics. He knew that the altar of sacrifice had been ignored in the heady hedonistic days of idol worship. Before the fireworks, the altar had to be restored. First the foundation stones were put in place. We have to do the same before the fire will consume our sacrifice. We must get our foundation right before we will see the fire that sets our hearts free.

To call down fire from heaven is a grave and dangerous thing. Fire is difficult to manage, and when it is sent from on high, it is impossible to contain. In the realm of the Spirit, fire always precedes the outpouring of His rain.

HAVE YOU EVER CALLED DOWN THE FIRE?

Elijah did…but he let the pagan priests have a shot at it first. They danced; they sang; they cut themselves silly. Blood flowed, but the fire did not. Elijah was a bit saucy, taunting those masters of deception while they worked up their fireless frenzy. Flames will not appear until you look to the Father of fire and the maker of rain.

Sacrifice. **Fire**. Rain. It all starts with the death of our idols. Letting go completely of what we hold most dear is a sacrifice that is pleasing and acceptable unto the Lord. A few years ago, I had to call down fire. And let me tell you, there is no greater pain than that of being burned alive. I still smell the smoke. When you look to heaven and ask to have your idol roasted, don't forget that the flames that destroy the idol you're clinging to will nearly consume you too. But the refining fire that scorches your heart will also bring deliverance.

We all have our idols. I just didn't realize how tightly I was holding on to mine. It was so big that every time God opened a door, my idol would get caught in the jamb. I wouldn't let go, and we couldn't go through. I am horrified to think of all the opportunities I missed to love someone in pain, to speak a word of hope to a desperate soul, or simply to be in a place of contentment with God. Instead I chose idol gain.

We are all subject to one of the big 3. Some fall for money, some fall for power, and others, like myself, fall for love. I loved love. What a Godlike thing the enemy used to enter my camp to consume my life, my passion, and my time. What an innocent thing I considered it to be, when in the end it nearly tore me apart. Even love can bring you to your knees when you elevate it to the place of idolatry.

I looked for love in all the wrong places, when the love I needed most was right there for the taking. God's love. But I wanted the all-consuming love found in another human being in the intoxicating days of a spring romance. I yearned for the love of a lifetime that would last as long and fill as much. But there is more beyond the here and now, and only the love of the one who made me could carry me into the ***there and then***. Eternally.

LOSE-LOSE PROPOSITION.

I was going to fight Him to the death on this one. The funny thing is, when you declare war on God, even if you think you win, you lose. His win, I thought, would mean death—to my dreams, to my passion, to my lifelong pursuit. But it was my win that would have meant death—physically and, ultimately, spiritually.

No matter where I went or what He called me to do, I had one eye scanning the landscape—in India, Hong Kong, Paris, and Prague—looking for the one. I searched for that yet-to-be-introduced individual who would carry me away to a place where goodness and love, safety and ecstasy would overcome all else. Sadly, while looking for that, I missed what I had.

Finally, just down the road, I found that love. It was my first real love, and the sheer intensity of it nearly consumed me. I had not known love could be so good. Still, something quiet, something subtle, yet something more powerful than this began to ache in a place I hadn't known to exist—the deep, hollow void that is left when the God of the universe has been displaced.

Because God is such a gentleman, you rarely hear Him go. He steps quietly to the sidelines, waiting for your dance with darkness to end so He can offer you new life again. But it isn't long before His absence and silence become louder than living your dream. I expected judgment, condemnation, and death. My actions deserved the worst, but He reserved the best. Even as I fearfully tightened my grip on my idol, I felt only waves and waves of His sweet love wrapped in grace. Somehow, above the din of the battle I waged in the pit of my own private hell, I heard the promise of an abundance of rain.

Funny how God works. He surprises us with goodness in the middle of our slow dance with death. He quietly taps death on the shoulder and asks to cut in. It is His kindness, not His wrath, that calls us to repentance. It was this love and compassion that brought me to my knees—and gave me the courage to look to heaven and call for fire.

WATER FIRE RAIN

Back to the drama high atop Mount Carmel. Before Elijah called down the fire, he acknowledged his complete and utter powerlessness in the precarious proceedings. He did this with water. He doused his sacrifice, altar, and wood. Not once, but three times. Nothing like raining on your own parade. But Elijah knew the truth: This was God's parade of power, not his.

Now if it had been me, I would have drenched the thing with gasoline from an Evian bottle and juggled torches just before I called to the heavens. But Elijah, no doubt a better man than I, made sure God remained in the spotlight. The prophet was there to raise the curtain and step aside so God could display His power.

Elijah set a good example for us. The water we pour on our sacrifice must be our complete acknowledgment that we are powerless to let go of it. Apart from God, we cannot. Only He can light the fire. Only He can extricate the idols from our hearts and our lives. Then the rain falls and new life begins.

I poured on the water, continuing to cling to my idol while my idol clung to me. Powerless and with a wavering voice, I called for fire—a call I wasn't even certain I wanted God to answer. The world seems to fall silent when someone calls to heaven for an all-consuming fire. I could have sworn the wrong party answered when the fire fell on cue. The four-alarm firestorm did not stop until every last vestige of my beloved idol had been burned from my heart and my hands. Another cry came from my lips. This one was a wordless and uncontrollable cry of pain as I stood blackened and bare in my pile of ashes.

Elijah saw the same sort of fire in God's pyrotechnical display. The waterlogged sacrifice and wood—even the stones—were completely consumed. There was nothing left but ashes. I know the feeling. God's fire is an awful thing, in the best sense of the word.

For Elijah, the children of Israel, you, and me, the story does not end there. Elijah ordered the deaths of the priests, since they might have lured the people back to idol worship.

You, too, must eliminate whatever would entice you to return to your idol. You must seal shut any doorway that would lead you back to an idol lifestyle. The priests that point to death must be executed to prevent another bout with fire. You know your priests. Maybe they are the films, music, or magazines that pave the way to the land of the false gods. Perhaps they are the cunning people who nudge you down the path of destruction. Or could they be pride and smug satisfaction with your own good works? The priests are robed in many clever clothes, and you must identify and kill them without further ado. And do. Elijah did. How about you?

AFTER THE FIRE

After reading about the pain, you may be thinking, *I don't want to be drenched and burned. I don't want to be left alone waiting for **what** in loveless despair. Besides, my heart is big enough for God and the objects of my desire.* I thought that way for a long time, but God showed me that He wanted me to belong to Him and Him alone.

And the story still doesn't end here. Joy always follows a season of crying, and rain always follows a fire of purifying.

Elijah sent a messenger to scan the sky above the sea. He saw only the promise of an **abundance of blue.** But after his seventh forced trip, the messenger's words were exactly what the tired prophet sitting on very dry ground was waiting to hear: On the horizon was a small cloud, the size of a man's pierced hand, with small drops of mercy gathering within.

If you listen, you will hear it, too—the same sound Elijah heard so many years ago. It was the sound I heard when my own fire subsided, and it is a sound you will hear if you close your eyes and open your heart. Disregard the long, dry season you've just endured. Set aside the pain of your personal firestorm. Close your eyes and listen—in that gathering of the clouds—listen to the sound of the promise of an abundance of rain.

REIgN. RAIN ON ME
WARM DROPS OF MERCY
TO SET MY HEART FREE.
RAIN ON ME, SWEET
JESUS, REIgN.
POUR DOWN YOUR
PROMISE AGAIN
AND AGAIN.

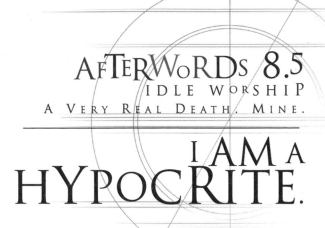

I AM A HYPOCRITE.

Until just now, I have been going through the motions, and I've been doing it with passion and conviction. Yet I have not gone all the way. I have spoken in spirit, but I have not been willing to move in the fullness of truth. I think that is a huge problem not just for me, but for all who claim to believe.

True worship of the one true God is the source of all real power. The joy of the Lord is our strength. Real joy comes when we worship the one who made us, despite how hard life may seem or how enslaved we feel to our sins. We must lift God to His proper place, robed in majesty on the throne of grace.

But the power has been out for too long, for reasons that are clear. We've been worshiping idols rather than God because we live in fear. We somehow have decided that God is not big enough to fix our problems or meet our needs. We have limited Him, and that is a form of idolatry. That kind of thinking says that I and my issues are bigger than God and His strength. By limiting Him, I limit me.

I told you about gang members who say that they cannot get out of their gang. That becomes true only because they believe it's true. As long as I believe that my particular problem, addiction, or sin is bigger than my God, then I am living in idolatry: I am bigger than God; He is smaller than me. In that form of idol worship, I am enslaved until I am willing to believe that God and His power are greater than my stuff, my sin, and me.

But sometimes it is our idle worship that robs us of His power. Idle worship can only cease when we worship in both spirit and in truth—the whole truth. If I claim to believe yet remain enslaved to things "bigger than the power of my God," I lie and have to live a lie by putting on a plastic face when I tell you I believe.

When we say one thing but do another, pain makes its face known. Often on our face. No matter how hard we try to convince others that we are happy or content, we are usually the only ones deceived. Though I claim to believe my God, the pain you see is real, so you might think the God I confess is not really real, or at least not powerful enough to take care of all of me.

One of the greatest problems in Christianity is that we often do not tell the truth about God and the truth about ourselves. We do not say loudly enough that God is a God of infinite love and compassion and that He is good and we are not. We have been lying about ourselves, and those on the outside of belief get the impression that

Christians think that they are good and better and without sin. That is the farthest thing from the truth, and we are robbed of His power when we do not worship in spirit and in truth.

For me, writing this book has been a form of worship. I am pouring out who I am and what I've come to know about God. That is a big part of what worship is—pouring out all we are before the God who made us. Until now, I wasn't sure I wanted to tell you the whole truth. But if I don't, my worship will be idle.

GROWING THROUGH THE MOTIONS

I'm learning that to avoid going through the motions, we must start *growing* through the motions. And because I'm the one who is writing this, I guess it will have to start with me.

To do so, I must tell the truth—to God, to you, to me. If we don't tell the whole truth, we remain enslaved in our dark, private prisons of pain, unable to help others whose fate is just the same. We are powerless, and we are framed.

The God of all love and all grace knows who we are, what we have done, and what we are capable of doing, yet His love remains the same. We are the only ones we deceive when we don't believe.

I have asked you to risk it all if you really believe. I promised that you would die a thousand deaths to who you are, to all your dreams, to all your fears, and to all you once believed. And I claimed that if you did, you and others like you would be free.

I believed that for you.

Now, I must believe it *for me.*

I have been afraid to tell the whole truth because somewhere along the line I decided what God, my friends and family, and you could handle. I would handle the rest. But I'm learning that in doing so, I will never know real rest. By not telling the whole truth, though I will offend no one, I will deprive the desperate ones who need it—desperate ones like me. Ninety-nine may take offense, but let this book be for the one lost sheep.

So here is the rest, though the telling feels like death.

The idol I cleverly disguised in the previous chapter had a name. More than just a name, this was and is a person—a sensitive and loving person who once cared, and may still care, deeply for me despite what I put him through. His was a name I feared to share. Not for fear that Mark would care, but for the fear that you would care. Or perhaps that after reading that single word, you would decide not to care. Then you would throw out all the other words because somehow my secret was worse than the one you have to share.

I cannot manage your emotions, and I cannot manage to convince you to feel anything other than what you feel. All I know is that as I have been challenging you to believe, God has been calling me to tell the truth of who I am and how He wants to set *all* captives free. Right now, I think He's working overtime on me.

For too long, too many voices have shouted, to the exclusion of everything else about Him, that God is an angry God and that those who break His laws will fry in the hottest of hells. But there is another hell as real as the one about which we have been told. It's the hell we create with the secrets we hold. And there are some secrets we hold because of the things we have been told or have not been told.

We've been told that certain sins, perhaps like the one I have shared, are worse than the ones you might be willing to say. But there is one thing I know: A sinner is simply one who has lost his way. Whether you have lost the way by a block or by a mile, you are not where you should be. That is what is important, not the brand, the style, or the depth of your place of need. We are all in a place of need. It is no real secret—God is what we need.

Despite what you may have heard, the God I've been telling you about is a God of love. It is His kindness, not His wrath, that draws us to repentance. Who comes running to an angry old man who is screaming furiously in judgment and rage? If you are at all like me, you will move freely toward only those who love freely. His love is truly free, and it is the truth of His love that sets the captives free.

Some Christians have made a big business out of guilt and shame. Too often, we have pointed out the sinner and focused on the sin, rather than pointing out the way to the God who loves, not the God who hates, to the God who cares, and the God who waits.

And He does, you know.

For God so loved that He gave. His son. And it was His son who took our pain—who took our place. Because of His blood and our belief in the Son, our sins have been erased. The one the Son sets free is free indeed. That goes for you, and it goes for me. It is true for all who will believe.

God asks us to come just as we are and allow Him to do with us as He will. I am strong in His strength only when I admit I am weak. I know that I cannot change. But in telling you the truth, in telling God the truth, I look to Him to make the change. I look to Him in the truth of who I am—and I look now without shame. I look to Him and find that I've no longer lost the way. That is all there is to say.

It is true: He requires purity; but that comes from Him, not us. When we open up and confess that which we have carefully hidden, as sons and daughters we are covered by His blood, and with that comes forgiveness.

CONFESS YOUR SINS TO EACH OTHER
AND PRAY FOR EACH OTHER
SO THAT YOU MAY BE HEALED.

www.james@5.16.com/niv

I know that if I had read these words when I needed them most, I may not have run long and hard from the one who loved me most. These words could have helped me believe beyond what I could see. But for too long, I couldn't believe because I didn't know the truth of who God is. I only knew the truth about me. Now, in telling you the truth and in sharing this, my final secret, I feel a heaviness begin to leave. That alone makes it easier to believe.

I don't have all the answers. I am not "fixed," but I'm learning to believe. The more I believe, the more freedom I see, and that keeps me moving closer to Him and farther from me.

Like my pit bull Erich, I may never understand why God has put certain boundaries and laws into place. I've asked Him a million times to explain Himself while I've tried so hard to work around Him and His fences. But I want to trust that He knows more than I do and that my loving Father wants to protect me from what I cannot see— from pain, from death, from heartache, and disease. Or maybe just those doggone fleas.

I knew that one day I would have to tell the world the truth—today I do, and today I'm closer to being free. And though I've said it before, I'll say it again (they are not my words; they're my best friend's): "You will know the truth, and the truth will make you free."

I will tell you what I know and nothing more. I am what I am, and despite what I thought, my God and His love are more than that. I stand naked before you, my God, and anyone who might wish to cast a stone. I feel safer in the light of the truth than I did in the dark with the secrets that I owned. I stand here now and I worship in spirit and in truth.

Idle worship turns to vital worship while my sins I now confess. In the telling and the dying comes real and total rest.

AND NOW YOU KNOW THE REST.

AfterWords 9.0

HE INHABITS THE PRAISES OF HIS PEOPLE.

He lives among us when we choose to praise Him. His strength is in us
when we raise Him—above what we see, what we know, what we feel,
where we go. Praise is taking a long, hard look at ourselves and our
situations, then, no matter what we see, holding the good, the bad, and
the ugly up before Him to say thanks—not only in our words, but also
in our deeds.

If you are anything like me, you probably have the hardest
time forgiving yourself. But the God who is perfect has looked past our
imperfections and has chosen not only to forgive us, but also to love
us—unconditionally until the end of time. We can hide nothing from
Him, so I wonder why we try. Only when we accept the fact that we are
screwed up can we worship as we live. As we love. And as we give.

GIVE AND IT WILL BE GIVEN.

Worship is an act of giving—recklessly giving back in passion, in acts,
in love, and in song. Not just a song, but the music of our lives—the

music of who we are and who we are going to be when we step into the fullness of belief and accept the plans He has for us. Worship in spirit and truth is dynamic: When we pour out ourselves before the God who made us, He can fill us up as we offer Him our praises.

But we can worship like this only when we're naked, as was the case with King David. David removed his royal robes in true humility, and so must we. We must strip ourselves of all the things that make us kings—those things that keep us from truly being free. Naked has nothing to do with what we are wearing; naked is the truth of who we are before the one who made us as we humbly offer up ourselves in real and vital praises.

DAVID DANCED IN HIS UNDERPANTS.

David was a man after God's own heart. As a young boy he was left alone at night with a big herd of sheep. I imagine that he felt down and outcast, out there alone in the fields and unable to sleep. But he learned the compassion of a shepherd from the maker of those sheep. There in a cold, dark place of solitude, David cried out for help, and lucky for him (and lucky for us), the Great Shepherd was not asleep. God heard the cries of one who longed for authentic love, and it was evident in David's praises.

David was out in the fields when God sent the prophet

Samuel to choose Israel's new king. After seeing Jesse's seven other sons, the prophet asked, "Are there more I have not seen?" How did David feel while his brothers auditioned for the part? The Old Testament does not tell us. All I know is that David's dad was not willing to put his youngest son forward as a candidate for king.

I gained insight into this kingly conundrum a few years ago while shooting a show in Jerusalem. In that ancient city, outside a vegetarian café, I had a strange and divine meeting with a harp maker named Ariel, who crafted harps like those David used to play. I had hired Ariel and her husband to re-create those harps and play them on our show. The day after filming, I ran into her on the street.

She rushed up to me, said a brief hello, and asked, "Do you know why David was a man after God's own heart?"

I shook my head, wondering why she wanted me to know. The Middle Eastern sights and smells of that ancient atmosphere gave Ariel's words a vividness that made her message clear.

"James," she said, as she looked deep into my eyes, "David was an outcast like you, but God was on his side."

She said that God is drawn to those whom others overlook. Being an outsider and an outcast, she said, stirs God's compassion like nothing else. David had learned compassion out there among the sheep, and it was his ability to love that caught the attention of the King of Kings. God chose David for his compassion, and that came from being an outsider—an outsider who was a lover and a fighter and an amazing songwriter. And it was this outsider who moved inside the palace to take his place as king.

"The process of becoming a person after God's heart is like making olive oil," Ariel continued. "The olives must first be crushed before the oil can come forth. We must first be crushed if we are going to move in love and compassion mixed with joy and with passion."

As a young boy David quickly learned what it has taken me far too long to learn: There is a love that can't be earned, a love that lasts, and a love that is real, for those who are willing to let themselves feel. And for those who will believe.

David believed. And David lived and worshiped like he believed—passionately, frighteningly, and radically. He lived and he loved with all of his heart, mind, and soul. He let go of what he could see and held on to what he had come to know.

God.

Although David's passion also led to sinning, his honesty was the key. In the end He stood naked before his King and owned his heinous deeds. The king danced naked before his King. God's blood atones and that set David free.

Idle worship becomes vital worship when we dance without pretense, pride, or masks before the one who made us. When we do, our lives become our praises. In living and loving freely, we see the power restored as the people are restored. But not before we are willing to pour ourselves out.

I think that dancing naked is a great visual metaphor for what God is looking for. When you dance naked, you let God and everyone else see just who you are. You say, "It doesn't matter how I may appear. It doesn't matter if you think I am fat, skinny, attractive, or repulsive. I am worshiping my Creator. I am looking past all that's ugly to accept that Jesus can love me. Just as I am. Just as you see. Just as we are—just to be free."

When we hide nothing from our God or from each other, we begin to move into that place of freedom where His life-changing power can enter our domain—where the supernatural can change us, our circumstances, and our pain. The joy of the Lord is our strength. Joy is what will bring us our strength, and joy cannot be manufactured. It is given when we offer up to Him our lives, just as He has given.

ALTHOUGH YOU MAY THINK IT SOUNDS A LITTLE BIT CRAZY, JESUS SAID IF YOU DON'T DO IT, THE ROCKS WILL PRAISE ME.

Vital worship is pouring ourselves out naked so the God of creation can fill us back up. In that filling comes joy and real power. But often things have to get bleak before we are willing to pour ourselves out.

RESTORE TO ME THE JOY OF YOUR
SALVATION, AND UPHOLD ME BY YOUR
GENEROUS SPIRIT. THEN I SHALL TEACH
TRANSGRESSORS YOUR WAYS,
AND SINNERS SHALL BE CONVERTED TO YOU.

www.psalm@51.12.com/nkjv

Read on. David, the greatest worshiper of all time, asked the God of the universe to forgive him for having sex with a married woman and then murdering her husband. These are high crimes, even in our perverse and violent times. But in that day, those crimes were not tolerated. Even kings and presidents would face a judgment day. The press would press for justice, and there would be a price to pay. A life for a life. Death for a death. Death for even illicit sex.

When it was all said and done, David said what he had done, and in doing so this man after God's own heart was set free. It is the same for you and the same for me. David loved God with all his heart. He wrote song after song about the greatness of the God he served. But when reality hit, and it became clear that he had done extremely wicked things, David didn't cease to sing. His music continued to flow. Only the lyrics were changed to correct the obdurate.

COMMUTE MY DEATH SENTENCE, GOD,

MY SALVATION GOD,

AND I'LL SING ANTHEMS TO YOUR LIFE-GIVING WAYS.

UNBUTTON MY LIPS, DEAR GOD;

I'LL LET LOOSE WITH YOUR PRAISE.

GOING THROUGH THE MOTIONS DOESN'T PLEASE YOU,

A FLAWLESS PERFORMANCE IS NOTHING TO YOU.

I LEARNED GOD-WORSHIP

WHEN MY PRIDE WAS SHATTERED.

HEART-SHATTERED LIVES READY FOR LOVE

DON'T FOR A MOMENT ESCAPE GOD'S NOTICE.

www.psalm@51.14–18.com/msg

GOD, GIVE ME A BROKEN HEART IF THAT IS WHERE YOUR HEALING CAN START.

David may not have felt like singing. His circumstances were such that he undoubtedly felt more like dying. I can relate. I know you can, too. None of us are free of guilt. The honest confession of who we are and what we've done can bring joy to both the person telling and the one being told. For in that divine moment of naked truth, we can see ourselves as we truly are—in need. And it is only then that we can look to the one who can meet that need—indeed.

Confessing our faults and shortcomings sets us all free because suddenly we realize there's really no difference between you and me. It is only in covering up that we deceive, and those to whom we lie feel more alone as they struggle with the reality of their own need and the horrible thought that they are alone in the dying.

David asked God not only to forgive him, but also to open his mouth in song. *Deliver me, then open my mouth so I can sing about how great You are. Because right now, I don't feel great and You don't feel great, but down deep, I know You are.*

I feel like a broken record. From the first page until now, I've hit that same refrain: If you don't believe, ask for the ability to believe. If you don't hear, ask. If you don't love, ask for it by name. If you've screwed up, why wouldn't you do the same?

EVERYONE WHO ASKS RECEIVES.

www.luke@11.10.com/nkjv

Our Father is a just and loving God who calls it like He sees it. If you are really honest, you know that He sees it. Everything. So why on earth would we hide? Where on earth could we hide? It must be stupid pride. Truth be told, the foul smell of our sin and our shame is nothing compared to the stench of pride. God hates it, and so do I.

WHY DO I STILL HAVE SO MUCH PRIDE?

It would have been so much easier to write this book if I could have led you to believe that I was someone special who could be a great role model, a media superhero with a direct line to God. Maybe even a 900 line.

That would have been great. But then who could relate?

God wanted me to tell the truth. He didn't want you to follow me. He wanted me to be honest so we both could be free to follow the only one worth following, the only true superhero—no matter what the media may want us to believe.

I believe that God wanted me to share a secret that is difficult to tell in order to give us the license we need to move outside the hell of self-righteous pride to a place of freedom where His goodness and grace sustains our lives.

If we are faithful and willing to confess our sins, He is faithful and willing to forgive those sins. In the confession, there is freedom, and in the freedom, there is joy. In joy there is strength, and in strength we must abide if we are hoping to survive.

Vital worship is honest worship. It is worship saying, "I am a mess, so God, take care of the rest. And the rest." It is worship that involves pouring out all of who we are and all of who we've been— then holding up what's left in emptiness so He can pour Himself back in. But first we must be empty of us and all the junk we think is us. Then and only then can we be full of Him and free of sin.

AND FREE TO FULFILL THE BOLD AND MAGNIFICENT DREAMS THAT COME FROM HIM.

AFTERWORDS 9.5

DANCING AND DREAMING IN THE REIGN.

WITHOUT A VISION THE PEOPLE PERISH.

I have talked about the drought that comes when we live in sin. I said it seems the land is parched, like our sin-drenched hearts, and it is my cry that the rain will begin again. Droughts do no end of damage as the land and people become dry and drier. Our lives, our shelves, and the land-scape look windswept, bleak, and barren, and for the life of us we don't know what to do. And for the life of us, we must know what to do.

WITHOUT THE RAIN PEOPLE PERISH.

We've all been told that if we don't learn from history, we are destined to repeat it. So let's go back in time to another period of drought to see if we can't glean wisdom from those who have gone before to know what we have in store. Because right now, there is nothing in our store. We are empty, dry, and brokenhearted, but that's the place where God can get started. That's the place we need to be to realize our desperate need.

Back again to the times of kings and prophets, of plagues and drought and hail. Like his mentor, Elijah, Elisha had a direct line to God. But like you and me, he was terribly human and very much in need. God directed him to a poor old widow and her sons who were in even more need. When it looked like she was going to lose everything, including the two boys she loved, the woman cried out to Elisha, "Your servant, my husband, is dead…and the creditor is coming to take my two sons to be his slaves."

The widow looked imploringly at Elisha, hoping that he could give her something—divine or otherwise—to ease the pain of losing all that she had left, which wasn't much. Lucky for her, God is in the business of setting captives free. Even captives-to-be.

WHAT DO YOU HAVE IN THE HOUSE?

Before God was going to do any sort of miracle, He first brought some people together who readily admitted the magnitude of their need. Elisha had nothing, and neither did the widow.

"What do you have in the house?" Elisha asked. This question had to have surprised her; it certainly surprised me. As the widow looked around, she was probably thinking, *Oh great, another greedy preacher wanting to rip me off with the promise that God will meet my need if I just dig a little deeper in my purse.*

But this story took a different turn. Elisha waited while the widow searched her house. All she came up with was a small jar of oil. Hearing from God, Elisha told her to take the oil and pour it into every jar and vessel she could beg or borrow.

I imagine that she thought the prophet was nuts. What good could it possibly do to go to all the neighbors and borrow a bunch of jars? His instructions must have seemed a ludicrous exercise of lunacy in light of the ounce of oil she had in her tiny jar. She would spend all the energy she could muster to round up the jars, just to dribble drops of oil into one of them. Besides, what would the neighbors think?

God doesn't seem to care what the neighbors think. He doesn't even seem to care what *we* think. He just asks us to believe. He asks us to pour ourselves out, so He can pour Himself in. God can be all that our jars can hold. Our lives and purposes are what He can mold. It was no different for the widow, the prophet, and her two boys—they were all required to pour themselves out if they really believed. And it's no different for you and me.

JARS ARE LIKE DREAMS.

Empty jars are like our lives and our dreams. A jar that is empty has little value, but a full jar has the potential to be of great value, depending on what's inside.

WITHOUT A DREAM, PEOPLE PERISH.

We all need dreams. We all need jars to hold our dreams, and we all must look toward heaven and ask the God of the universe to give us those dreams that He wishes us to have to make our lives complete.

God asks us, just as He asked Elisha and the widow, to pour out whatever we have in our jars so He can pour Himself in and fill us up with dreams. But first comes the painful pouring out—the painful need to believe—before we can ever truly receive.

And it was no different for Jesus—if you can believe it.

Before God could fill the dreams and lives of all mankind, He first asked His only Son to be lifted up on the cross, naked and bare before pagans and priests, before judges and thieves, before you, before me. It was in that dirty and humbling place that the blood He poured out cleansed the whole human race. His *pouring out* allowed the *filling up* of our lives, our jars, and our dreams—no matter how obscene that vile, bloody scene may have seemed. It was this pivotal moment of naked worship—when the King of all Kings could be seen in bare humanity—that the God above all gods could set the captives free. Including you, including me.

IF ONLY WE BELIEVE.

Are you willing to pour yourself out? Are you willing to tell your darkest, most frightening secret to those you love, or to those you don't even know, to allow them to really get to know the you that you would love them not to know? If you are or if you do, you will be naked before the King. You will be naked before you sing. Like David, and like me, you must then ask Him to help you sing. Because real worship doesn't come naturally in that place of vulnerability. But whoever asks will most definitely receive. And all that He asks is for us to believe.

And then believe that you are free.

FULL FRONTAL LUNACY

It feels crazy to be that naked, but here we are, our souls stripped bare, worshiping out in the streets. I imagine that this is quite a spectacle for all the world to see. But it's a far more honest spectacle than the ones we've been forced to see—the ones where God has been misrepresented, misinterpreted, and misplaced, *Praise the Lord,* so pious pretenders can take the lead. I believe it's time for God to lead. I believe He's dying to lead. And I am dying when I allow Him to lead. But in the dying comes the thing that makes me free. In the pouring out of all that I am, there is the filling up of all that He is, and in this real life filling I find real joy, and I find real living. And the joy of the Lord is my strength.

In the jar of the Lord is our dream.

The widow and her sons filled their house with every jar and vessel they could find, and then she closed the door. "What do you have in the house?" How far will you go when you truly believe? This old widow went the last mile and filled every last jar with her one-ounce vial. Elisha told her to go out and sell the oil to pay her debts and use what was left to live out her final days in rest.

AND NOW SHE HAS AND KNOWS THE REST.

What do you have in the house? Are you willing to pour it all out? If you do, you will see miracles only believers can see. You will hear music like you've never heard before. You may be a fool, but you will be full, and you will be free.

Maybe we need to need more before we will actually see more. In that place of need, we can bring our empty vessels, jars, visions, and dreams—no matter how many or how few, how much or how little we may have. If we pour ourselves out in our lives and in our praise, the rocks can sit idly by.

↑UP↑ON THE ROOF

Some finals notes. A bunch of us meet in my glass loft on the rooftop of the old Pabst Brewery on Sunday nights. God shows up and fills our jars as we grow more willing to pour ourselves out. Last Easter, I spoke about this subject—how jars are like dreams—and I witnessed a more powerful resurrection than I have ever seen. My friend Chris, the worship leader of this loft church, looked around the room at all the young people who had gathered under the stars. He saw the potential of these youthful jars filled with vivid dreams.

As he looked into the eyes of everyone in the studio, he asked, "What do we have in the house? We have my son, a thirteen-year-old who knows three chords on the guitar. We have Jon, a young musician with carpal tunnel syndrome who can use his finger to play a note or two on the piano. We have a rhythmically-challenged *djembe* player"—that would be me—"and we have an assortment of voices and talents throughout this room. Are we willing to believe?"

Chris then asked those he pointed out to come forward and lead worship with whatever it was we had in the house—no matter how meager it seemed. I can tell you that I have never experienced worship more vital, more alive, more real than I did that night in that city of angels—in that city of broken dreams.

There in that loft on that old rooftop, I heard music like I have never heard before. The joy of the Lord was our strength. And although this was a new song, never sung before, I heard the voices of those around me blend and weave as we made up lyrics and rhythms and rhymes as we all moved together in time…

in the unpretentious nakedness of our belief.

ENTERTAINING ANGELS UNAWARE
IN OUR UNDERWEAR.

I believe angels joined our new song. I have never felt so strong as I sang words that filled my mind, words that had never been written down, words moving in rhyme—and those around me seemed to shine. Believe it or not, the new song was sublime.

I want to live like that until the end of time. I want to pour myself out and sing brand new lines. I want the God of the universe to fill me up as I pour myself out—as He fills us up, as we move together in our nakedness toward Him, hiding nothing from the one who knows no sin, who is not shocked by the depth of our sin. The one who will forgive and forever forget if we only ask Him. Hiding nothing from the one who sees through jars and through our skin to our hearts and our dreams and all that we've been.

God, I want my idle worship to turn to vital worship, so pour me out and pour You in.

We can only be strong in Him when we admit to one another that we are weak. And we can only do that when we truly believe.

GOD, HELP ME BELIEVE.

AfterWords 10.0
SUBLIME SUBVERSION
This Is A Cry For Total REVOLUTION

FOR THOSE WITH EYES TO SEE, LET THEM SEE.
FOR THOSE WITH EARS TO HEAR,
LET THEM HEAR.

Real revolution begins when we understand that what we see is not necessarily what we should believe. By looking beyond the tangible and visible, we see with the eyes of God into the realm of belief, the realm of what can be. This revolution begins not with weapons of our making, but with lives lived out in real and vital praising.

NEO, THE WORLD AS YOU SEE IT IS REALLY NOT REAL.

The world in which we live is not as it appears. Ours is a fallen world that has been highjacked by an artificial intelligence that has learned to play us off against our fears. We have been duped into believing that all that is real is what we can see.

The system as we know it prevents us from truly living free. The slavery is sometimes obvious and involves tangible chains. But

the most deadly bondage of all is the bondage we can't see—the one
that keeps us from our purpose and our God, who makes our dreams
and destinies.

This world is all about slavery and keeping us in check.
Oppressed and powerless people consuming the opiates of the culture
make few waves while they feed the things that keep them all enslaved.
Too many of us have fallen in step and fallen behind. If we are not
careful, we may fall too far and feel no fear. Please ask God for eyes to
see and ears to hear.

FEAR NOT, FOR I AM WITH YOU...

BRING OUT THE BLIND PEOPLE WHO HAVE EYES,

AND THE DEAF WHO HAVE EARS....

LET THEM HEAR AND SAY, "IT IS TRUTH"...

THAT YOU MAY KNOW AND BELIEVE ME.

www.isaiah@43.5, 8–10.com/nkjv

For many of us, it is difficult to believe in light of all the
injustices that have been done in the name of religion and of the name
above all names. And it's easy to point a finger of accusation when we
ourselves have been accused. It is easy to point fingers; we do it all the
time. We all need excuses for why we don't believe, so we point to all

the hypocrites to justify our unbelief.

Usually we start with the addicts and crazies. Then we point at all those things that keep us all in slavery. We point at prisons, politicians, evangelists, and priests. We point at talk show hosts, lawyers, policemen, and thieves. Then we point at the pious, the powerless, the gurus, the sages—the rest homes, the restless homes, and all those earning wages. We point at Catholics, Baptists, Buddhists, and Jews. You could point at me, and I could point right back at you. But in all this pointing we miss the point. And the pointing leads to shooting, and shooting leads to death.

REVOLUTIONS OFTEN FAIL BECAUSE TOO MUCH BLOOD IS SHED.

If we are looking for a real revolution, we must look past what has been and point instead to Him, the perfect one who bled to set us free and give us bold new dreams and destinies.

This, my friends, is a new way to live. To start a revolution, be willing to forgive.

GIVE AND IT SHALL BE GIVEN. FORGIVE AND IT SHALL BE FORGIVEN.

If we are truly going to live a revolution, we will have to forgive all the pollution that has kept us in the dark and away from Him, the one who can show us how to forgive. Forgive the ones who did you wrong—forgive and He'll give you a brand new song. He who was unjustly accused, when He looked down from His tree at those Romans and Jews, didn't use His hands to point—He used his hands to bleed as He spoke words of forgiveness born of love:

"FATHER, FORGIVE THEM, FOR THEY KNOW NOT WHAT THEY DO."

A revolution began that fateful day. As His blood was shed, there was a price to pay. **It was paid.** Forgiveness came as He forgave. The model has been set—He has shown the way. It worked back then, and it works today.

Forgive those who have neglected, abandoned, and abused. Forgive those who didn't love you; forgive those who used. Forgive the missing fathers; forgive the ones who stayed. Forgive the broken mothers and the ones who said they prayed. Forgive the friends who loved you and those who have betrayed. Forgive the crimes that have been committed in the name above all names.

Finally, forgive yourself for all the crimes you have committed in order to survive—for the times you ached and the times you lied, for the times you hid to protect your pride. Forgive yourself, and you are closer to living free—free from condemnation, past offenses, and desolate destinies.

Freedom to forgive begins when we're willing to believe.

For revolution to begin, we must have eyes to see and ears to hear. We must question what we've been told, and we must question what we fear. We cannot trust all those who have done this stuff before. We can only trust the one who stands knocking at our door.

I STAND AT THE DOOR AND KNOCK

There is one who asks you to believe. Although I've been doing all the talking, the one who's asking isn't me. He's the one who has been loving you from the start. I believe that He's just used me to help open up your heart. For the one who loved so much is the one who sets us free from bondage, chains, and curses—and ravaged destinies.

This is the Savior named Jesus—the only name that can set the captives free. It is a name you can accept or reject—but He's knocking at your door. No matter what you think or feel, it's one name you can't ignore. For more options, press none. That is not an option. For one day, every knee will bow and every tongue will confess that Jesus Christ is Lord. Don't you think it would be better to do it now, while He's knocking at your door?

The God of the universe has given all He can to show us that this life is not an accident. He has always had a plan. We are duped when we believe that the things we see are what we must believe. The things that we doubt may be the things we should believe.

I'm asking you to stop and drop all that you have, all that you know, and all that you think you are or who you might have been. Look beyond the here and now to the there and then. Look to the one who stands knocking at your door—to the one who made all that is, all that was, and all that is in store. The one who loves you most can do anything at all—except He cannot love you more.

By embracing this gentle God of love and trusting that He wants to be our friend, we will see real revolution lived out in the end.

UPRAY UWANT A REVOLUTION.

There is nothing pacifistic about any of this. This isn't a trendy book with tips on how to live a pleasant and prosperous life. As far as I'm concerned, that's preposterous and trite. This is a call for a revolution, and it will cost you your whole life.

A strange kind of war ensues when you take up the call of the revolution. Love is the banner, sacrifice is supreme, and living comes through dying. Are you going to put your faith in a system that enslaves? Or are you willing to believe those nuts with great big signs that read embarrassingly "Jesus Saves"?

Because He does, you know.

He saves all those who are willing to believe. He saves them from the darkness of dismal destinies. His is the only name on earth that can set the captives free. Strangely, His is the only name we're not allowed to use on regular TV.

What's up with that?

THE KINGDOM OF HEAVEN SUFFERS VIOLENCE, AND THE VIOLENT TAKE IT BY FORCE

www.matthew@11.12.com/nkjv

There has never been a figure in all of history who lived so short a time on earth yet changed the course of so many who have chosen to believe. His name has divided kingdoms, families, and friends. His name is the name above all names and will remain until the end. Although somehow along the line, His name has been placed in placid obscurity, when the truth of that name is linked to violent change, just saying it makes demons flee. Jesus lived a revolution, and His dying fed the flame. I think He's asking us to believe so our lives will do the same.

REACT

Until now, I have lived like a reactionary. I have not liked televangelists, religion, and most churches where I've been. As much as I think I don't, I still make great distinctions between *us* and *them.* I don't act; I react, and I certainly don't revolutionize. But the simple truth is this: Jesus Christ was and is the greatest revolutionary who ever lived. His life and all that He embodied opposed a system that enslaves. He worked for the good of the people, and His life He freely gave.

He is asking us to do the same.

FREEDOM FIGHTERS

Jesus was a freedom fighter, and He continues to set captives free. He sometimes does it in an instant and other times it's step by step, which seems to be the case with me. Our only role is simply to believe. And we don't even have to have the capacity. We need only ask the one who can help us to believe.

The world has seen many freedom fighters give their lives to set captives free, and it doesn't take a genius to see that the system is not friendly to those who fight for liberty.

William Wallace fought mightily for Scotland, though at times it seemed he was alone. The others were so full of fear, they cut and ran back home. But Wallace put his life on the line for the greater good, and the good just got greater after his blood was shed. His blood ran out long before his resilience did. As a result of the life he freely gave, his people followed his example and determined to be free.

Abraham Lincoln tried to break the chains of slaves, and a

bullet put him in the grave. Martin Luther King Jr. had a dream to do the same, and at the risk of sounding like a broken record, a bullet put him in the grave. Sung and unsung heroes of cultures, countries, and tribes have given it all, including their lives, to bring the truth to people enslaved by the system's clever lies.

If you haven't gotten it by now: The system is not our friend. It will not be, and it has never been. Yet when you learn to hear God's voice and let go of your will, you'll be surprised by the sublime subversion that brings victory and freedom to a people oppressed—to us as well as them.

You will have to make a choice, you know. And if you choose the red pill instead of the blue pill, one day you'll lose your voice. And your life. Freedom fighters never seem to last until Act III, but what matters isn't the length of our lives or the measure of our success—it's what we've lived to be. And if we have lived in the fullness of His freedom for just a minute or a year, that is far greater than a long life lived in fear.

YOU HAVE A DESTINY.

We are called to be agents of change. God designed us to break out of our chains, and from our freedom He calls us to bring freedom to the masses. Freedom to all we meet in all cultures and all classes. Our God is an equal opportunity employer, and He asks us to be bold and mighty warriors. There is a revolution that is about to begin. There is a war that will be waged, and we must fight it till the end.

LIVING, LOVING, FORGIVING AND DYING, AND LIVING ALL OVER AGAIN.

AfterWords 10.5
PAYING vs. PLAYING
WITH YOUR LIFE
That's one L of a Difference

Real revolutions, as romantic as they seem, always carry a high price. I believe you can do pay-per-view (fighting skirmishes here and there) or you can pay with your whole life.

DIE NOW
OR PAY LATER...

Before my eyes and with all my senses, I have witnessed two powerful depictions of revolutions. Both stirred in me an insatiable desire to live with all the passion my heart could push through this mortal coil. Both made me leap to my feet with tears streaming down my face as the music swelled and the passion poured lavishly on the stage. But only one of them embodied real revolution—social, personal, and full-blown spiritual rebirth. Blood was shed and lives were lost, but there was redemption in the end.

That production was *Les Miserables.* In it, Jean Valjean

commits a minor crime in order to survive. Judgment is swift and severe, and Valjean is sentenced to many years of hard labor for simply stealing bread. Even after he pays his debt, under the law Valjean is forever a criminal, a number, an enemy of the state. Despite the fact that he has changed—a change brought about by an undeserved act of mercy by a forgiving priest—he runs from his accuser his entire life. His personal battle rages until his accuser no longer remains, and at last Jean Valjean finds redemption he can claim.

The other production was the Pulitzer Prize-winning *Rent*. The music still runs through my mind, and when it does, I feel the emotions swell all over again. There on that passion-drenched stage I witnessed the pain and the power of a generation in the throes of a pseudorevolution. The intent of this revolution is to secure individuality in a system that screams for conformity and "same" and the personal freedom to live like there is no day but today. Like real revolution, this one, too, is fought to the death.

I watched *Rent*'s accidental criminals—the neglected, the abandoned, the abused, the ignored—run from their accuser while they screamed and danced and sang and loved as if there were no tomorrow—as if there were only today. In just a few short hours, I witnessed the death of a beautiful Angel and the birth and resurrection of love lost and found again. I watched a drug addict nearly die of AIDS and find a new lease on life again.

I sang along. I know the pain. I felt the love and I cling to the refrain: 525,600 minutes—all the moments that make up a year. The sunrises, the sunsets, the laughter, and the tears. How do you measure a year? How do you measure a life? The cast swelled in one voice that nearly brought me to my knees.

HOW ABOUT LOVE?

As much as I love the passion of *Rent,* I can't help but tally the sum of all that is spent for that which cannot be kept, but only lent. A temporary lease to live in personal freedom for the moment mixed with joy and pain. But the price we pay to live in this temporary place of personal space seems far too great in terms of money, pain, and death—in terms of emptiness and regret.

Too many Angels are dying. Too many friends of all those angels are left crying. And we keep on paying that exorbitant rent till all we have is finally spent. And there we are, with nothing left.

As I watched this musical revolution for personal freedom and acceptance, I felt the blood stir in my veins. I wanted to leap to the stage and at the top of my lungs sing about today. To sing about now and the rent we all must pay to a system that enslaves. As the curtain fell and the cast took their final bows, I wanted to rush forward and throw my arms around every damaged member of that insanely talented crew.

I wanted to remind them that they are loved and accepted—that they always have been (and always will be) for each of the 525,600 minutes in each of the years that each has lived. I wanted to tell all those who had forgotten their Father and the way He intended for them to live and about all the love He has to give. For free.

For you.

For me.

HOW ABOUT LOVE?

How about love? What is it about love that brings such pain? That hides such pain? That makes so much pain worthwhile? All of the characters in *Rent* (and most of the characters in life) are looking for love, crying, and ultimately dying for the same—while hoping beyond death someone will remember their name.

WE'RE DYING IN AMERICA TO COME INTO OUR OWN...

Love and forgiveness are at the center of real revolution. But in *Rent,* too much is spent on that which cannot be sustained. Personal freedom, which demands so high a price, is only borrowed, not retained. And no matter how powerfully the music swells, in the end the curtain falls, and we are all left alone to face that bright light—the light that the character named Angel faced as he/she walked softly into that dark night. Alone.

In the end, all of us must face death alone.

Walk boldly into that sweet light, and you will hear the old refrain: If the Son sets you free, you will be free indeed. And you will know the truth, and the truth will make you free. In believing this, you will lose your chains, forget your pain, and gain a brand new eternity.

HE'S LIKE SON I MIGHT'VE KNOWN...

Ever since I read Hugo's *Les Miserables* and then witnessed it on the stage, I have been dying to give my life for something I could believe in with all my heart. I hoped that some sort of revolution would begin in my lifetime so I could join a triumphant group of young warriors and charge into battle singing powerful songs without fear. Without shame.

The revolution has begun, whether you know it or not. The battle has been waging through the centuries, and if we open our eyes and open our hearts (and maybe even a vein), we will be a part of a triumphant new day. A triumph born of revolution, so there won't be hell to pay.

My friend Terry, who is from South Africa, pointed out that true revolution is not just taking what is and turning it upside down. That's what pseudorevolution is—that and nothing more. Though the rulers may change, the slavery and oppression remain the same. Only the presidents are changed to restrict the impotent.

Real revolution is powerful and dynamic. The point is to set captives free. But to move in might and power, first we must be set free. For that, we must believe.

Real revolution moves forward the truth we have come to embrace. Imagine a wheel spinning: It turns upside down as it revolves and then turns upright once again. But the goal is the moving forward, not the turning upside down. I believe that as we share the truth with each other about our God and our lives, we will experience a revolution for all time. We must move forward with the truth and forward with our lives.

REVOLUTION, THEN, IS PROGRESS. AND NOTHING IS CONTRIVED.

As you may have guessed from my last name, my heritage is French, so revolution runs naturally in my blood. But the sort of revolutions my forefathers led ended up shedding too much blood. In the end, after too much death and a pretty ugly mess, the people remained oppressed.

TEMPORAL FREEDOM VS.
ETERNAL FREEDOM

Taking part in a revolution is a messy and dangerous business. Whether you are fighting for a temporal, personal freedom, or a freedom that redeems, you are taking a great risk. In truth, you may have no day but today.

Johnathan Larson, a personal freedom fighter and the creator of *Rent,* did not get to see the curtain go up on his Tony Award-winning play—that moving and magical dream that screams *carpe diem,* **seize the day!**

Though Johnathan did just that, there was a price he had to pay. On the night before the preview performance, his heart seized on that, his final day. No day but that day. He did not live to see his work win the accolades, praise, and support of all the people who harmonized with his pain. He never heard the masses sing his haunting last refrain: 525,600 minutes—how do we measure a year—a life—Tonys, ovations, in Pulitzer Prizes—in sunsets, in laughter, in life's grand surprises?

HOW ABOUT LOVE?

Jesus said they will know us by our LOVE. Today, it seems too many Christians are known by their hate—their judgment and the pain they inflict on all those who do not sing along with their glad refrain, "Onward Christian soldiers, marching as to war."

And there will be a war, a culture war, if we forget the core of what Jesus said, how He lived, and what He has in store. Love and forgiveness cover a multitude of sins. It is not too late for any of us. Now is the time to begin. Begin by learning to forgive.

WILL YOU JOIN OUR REVOLUTION?

When we join the revolution, a revolution of forgiveness born of love, we will achieve the goal of ultimate redemption, as we boldly sing that same refrain:**525,600 minutes** lived in love and shared with those in so much need, in so much pain. And when we give of ourselves and pour ourselves out, we will find that our revolution has begun. For each of us personally and for all of society. But it would cost us all our lives—if our Father had not already paid the price.

In our revolution, we are like Jean Valjean in *Les Miserables*. We are all under the law, being stalked by the specter of death for the crimes of survival many of us have committed. Some were inflicted on us, and some we've brought on ourselves, but the results are just the same. We keep running; we keep dying; all the while we keep lying to hide the things that keep us all enslaved.

We are being hunted and hounded by the avenger of blood, and his greatest weapon is our own unnecessary shame and the secrets we hold safely locked inside our brains. Will we keep on the run and continue to hide while we mask mountains of pain hidden deep in our pride?

For us, as for Jean Valjean, redemption comes in the end

through an undeserved act of mercy by our own High Priest—Jesus. It can be owned for now, for the moment, and the 525,600 minutes that follow in each subsequent year. And the redemption is owned, not rented or leased, and will carry us just as He carries us, gently into that dark night. And the darker it gets and the deeper we go, the closer we move to His pure light.

Can you hear the people sing...Revolution, real revolution, begins when we are willing to forgive. In truth, there is nothing we can do about how others choose to live and how their choices cause us pain. But in the act of forgiveness, you can join that last refrain. For the blood of the one who was without sin has washed your sin away.

Yes, we have today.

And when we stop paying rent and pay with our lives by letting go and trusting Him (the one who paid the greatest price), freedom, dignity, and redemption will remain.

FOR NOW. FOREVER
AND ESPECIALLY FOR TODAY.

For those with eyes to see, let them see. For those with ears to hear, let them hear. This is a call for revolution and a call for freedom fighters who make revolutions reality. It only takes a single decision—the decision to B E L I E V E.

You can make that decision any time, but as Johnathan
Larson learned, and so powerfully proclaimed, THERE IS

N O   D A Y
BUT TODAY.

AfTeRWoRDs 11.0
THE REST OF HIStory

NOW WE WHO HAVE BELIEVED ENTER THAT

REST, JUST AS GOD HAS SAID.

www.hebrews@4.3.com/niv

This is the culmination. This is where we finally let go and let Him into every aspect of our lives. This is the moment when we finally decide. This is when we have to cast our doubts aside. I believe this is the time.

If you want to know the rest of this story, you may have to wait around several years. The truth is that many of the things I've shared—the words and promises of an invisible God—have not yet come into their fullness of being. I see them even though I'm not really seeing.

I have caught only a glimpse of greater things to come. Though I need a lot of work, I know it can be done. I know it is being done.

THERE REMAINS THEREFORE A REST FOR THE

PEOPLE OF GOD. FOR HE WHO HAS ENTERED

HIS REST HAS HIMSELF ALSO CEASED FROM HIS

WORKS AS GOD DID FROM HIS.

www.hebrews@4.9–10.com/nkjv

NO MORE WORKS.

I'm tired of pretending. I'm tired of trying. Something tells me, though, that I'm not through with dying. But I am confident of this very thing: He who started a good work is faithful to complete it. I want to be faithful to complete my part. And that requires belief.

This world is not friendly to those who choose to believe. The clock always seems to be ticking for those who work to set the captives free. But the one who loved the most was willing to die, so why then shouldn't we?

There is little glory in taking this path. The battle is real, and many men die. But take comfort in this: We are not alone. There is a great cloud of witnesses—men and women who have believed. They went before in great sacrifice and pain, but the fruit of their lives is still fragrant today.

AND THEIR BLOOD HAS MARKED THE WAY.

There isn't time enough to tell of all those who have gone before—that great company of men and women who willingly embraced what they could not see while they believed what was in store. For they heard their God speak. That was enough, even if they died before they could see.

In their willingness to believe, this great cloud of witnesses subdued kingdoms, obtained promises, stopped the mouths of lions, and quenched the violence of fire—even on the martyr's pyre. Some escaped the edge of the sword, while others died on that edge while trusting in their Lord. In their weakness, they were strong, and in their living and their dying, they learned a brand new song.

They were valiant in battle—warriors of light. They turned back armies and watched the dead come back to life.

Some were tortured, others mocked in kangaroo courts—yet they chose to believe a much better report. Even chains of bondage could not keep their souls bound. For they believed the promise of their God and in them, faith was found. Some were stoned and tortured; others were sawn in two. They were tempted, tried, and tested, and beaten black and blue. But whether they were able to see or not to see, these, the faith-filled warriors, decided to believe. And in the believing came the freedom. And it was freedom they could see.

SINCE WE ARE SURROUNDED BY SO GREAT A CLOUD

OF WITNESSES, LET US LAY ASIDE EVERY WEIGHT,

AND THE SIN WHICH SO EASILY ENSNARES US,

AND LET US RUN WITH ENDURANCE

THE RACE THAT IS SET BEFORE US, LOOKING UNTO

JESUS, THE AUTHOR AND FINISHER OF OUR FAITH.

www.hebrews@12.1–2.com/nkjv

This is the world as best I remember it. Some may find it hard to believe. But I want to enter His rest so I can see how this ends. No matter how difficult it all may seem.

I don't know the rest of the story. But I do know that rest is His story. Storms may rage and the waves may swell while Jesus gently sleeps. But He invites us to rest nestled close to Him. He asks us only to believe.

I've gone way out on this limb. I guess I'm asking you to do the same. I hope it supports the weight.

And the wait.

To publish now, before I see how this ends, may be crazy,

I really believe.

God, help me believe.

I've asked it before. I'll ask it again.

What kind of fool believes?

ONLY A FOOL FOR CHRIST'S SAKE.

Would you like to walk this out with me?

Road trips are a lot more fun in the company of friends.

Together we'll discover how this journey called BELIEVE begins.

AND HOW IT NEVER REALLY ENDS.

N O   M O R E   W O R D S.

| T H E | B E G I N N I N G. |

Introduce yourself @ Godcom.com

I want to hear your thoughts and

experiences on this journey called

" B E L I E V E "